Table of Con

Foreword

A foreword to the book by Anna Coulling

Introduction to volume price analysis

A brief overview and introduction to the broad concepts of volume price analysis.

Section One - Daily charts

In this first section of the book we start with the daily timeframe for spot currency pairs.

All of these use the NinjaTrader platform, and regardless of whether you are in intraday trader or a longer term swing or trend trader, the daily chart is an excellent one for context based on the previous day's price action and volume. Comparing volume is more straightforward here as we have no session crossover issues to address, and so we are always comparing like with like. However, we do have to remember the seasonal aspect of volume, and take account of any public holidays, which will always be reflected in the associated volume.

Section Two - Hourly charts

In the second section of the book we move to consider the hourly timeframe. We stay with the spot market, but have changed platforms to MT4. Here we are now dealing with the issue of the session crossover and so must always consider comparing volume with like volume in the associated session. In other words, London with London and not London with the Far East and Asia session. Volumes do vary dramatically from one session to another, and here I explain how to consider the hourly chart and once again to compare like with like across the sessions.

Section Three - 15 minute charts

In this section we stay with the MT4 platform and spot forex examples for the 15 minute timeframe. But again we do still have to be careful when moving from one session to another, from the Far East and Asia, to London and then into the US. At each stage we have to pause the wait for the candles and volume to build. That said, we can also compare these over a longer period on the chart, and so compare a new session with a previous session from the day before.

Section Four - 5 minute charts

In this section we stay with the MT4 platform and spot forex examples for the 5 minute time-frame. Again we have to be careful here in the crossover from one session to another, from the Far East and Asia, to London and then into the US. At each stage we have to pause the wait for the candles and volume to build. That said, we can also compare these over a longer period on the chart, and so compare a new session with a previous session from the day before.

Section Five - 4 hour charts

In this section we move back to the slower timeframe of the four hour chart, and again the MT4 platform. This can be a tricky timeframe, as once more we have to make sure we compare like with like in terms of volume across the various sessions, but in some ways this is easier here, as we have several sessions on one chart.

Section Six - Currency futures

In the final section we move to a different instrument and platform and consider examples from the world of currency futures, by using the NinjaTrader platform once more. Here we are considering volume from the aspect of the big operators. But volume is volume, and as you will see from these examples across various timeframes, is equally powerful for a very different instrument. Volume here is the 'true' volume of futures contracts traded through the central exchange, but if you compare this with the proxy volume of the spot forex world, you will be surprised at how closely the two correlate.

Foreword

By Anna Coulling

Welcome to this book on examples of volume price analysis for forex trading, which I hope you enjoy reading and find useful, either to underpin your existing knowledge of this approach, or perhaps to introduce it to you as a new concept and methodology.

What I have tried to do in this book is to illustrate as many of the volume price analysis or 'VPA' concepts as possible using examples from both the spot forex and currency futures market, over a wide variety of timeframes, from the longer term charts to shorter intra day examples. I decided from the outset not to add any indicators or notations to the charts, but focus purely on the relationship between volume and price. But as you may already know from my other books, volume price analysis also embraces support and resistance, candles and candle patterns. However, I felt in creating this book of examples, I wanted to focus on the first principles of the volume price relationship itself, and to explain each example with simple and clear annotations.

In addition, I also wanted to demonstrate how this approach applies equally, whether you are a longer term swing or trend trader, a scalping trader intraday or even an investor in currencies for the longer term.

Each page has one chart with a description of the key points below, and whilst most are taken from the spot forex market, I have also included some examples at the end of the book for currency futures.

The charts are grouped by timeframe, but as I'm sure you appreciate, the concepts of volume price analysis apply in any market and in any timeframe. So whilst a weekly chart may have an example of a test or accumulation and distribution, the same principle will apply equally to a five minute or hourly chart for either spot of future.

I hope you enjoy studying the examples, and if this is a new and fresh approach to trading you might find my first book, A Complete Guide To Volume Price Analysis, helpful in explaining all the concepts and ideas from first principles, which will then help to give you a deeper understanding of the examples covered here.

Please note I use the terms market makers, insiders, big operators freely throughout the book. Where I use the term insiders it simply means just that - either market makers or big operators. In other words, those groups on the inside who manage and manipulate the markets.

Remember too that all the examples here are based on a single timeframe chart, and I would suggest you also apply a multiple time based approach to view the price action and volume analysis across the time horizon.

In addition I've also included the key indices that play an important part in any analysis, such as the dollar index, the yen index and the euro index, which then provide a view of the currency against a basket of others.

Relational analysis also plays a part in forex, with volume price analysis in related markets helping to provide a three dimensional view.

And I cannot stress too strongly that in order to become proficient in using the volume price analysis methodology takes practice, time and effort, and suggest you use a fast chart for practice, such as a five or fifteen minute chart, in any market, as this will allow you to study and learn in real time. The lessons of volume price analysis are universal and apply to all markets, which is why I have included them all here - to simply make this point. And if you have read any of the public reviews on Amazon, then you will be able to see for yourself how this approach has changed the lives of many traders and investors, who were struggling, perhaps not moving forward, but have now revolutionized their trading and investing having read my first book. And perhaps more importantly many of these traders and investors simply integrated this methodology into their existing approach, which has resulted in helping them see the markets clearly from the perspective of the insiders, so increasing their confidence and chart reading.

I hope you too will join these traders yourself, and regardless of whether you are a newcomer to investing and trading, or you are a more seasoned professional with years of experience, volume price analysis has something for everyone.

Wishing you every success and good fortune in your own trading journey, and I hope volume price analysis will form the cornerstone of your own trading methodology now and in the future.

Thanks again and best wishes - Anna Coulling

Introduction to volume price analysis

For many traders and investors, price and the price chart itself are the beginning and the end of technical analysis, and this perhaps best describes those traders who classify themselves as price action traders. All they consider is the price and nothing else. However, for myself, and many others, this approach completely ignores the extension of price to its logical association with volume, which together then reveals the truth behind the raw data of price.

The explanation generally given is that technical analysis is based on the underlying philosophy that all market sentiment is contained within a simple price chart. That a price chart encapsulates the views of every market participant at a given moment in time. Moreover, that technical analysis is simply price analysis, and that traders can forecast the future direction of price by analysing and studying where it has been in the past.

And whilst this is undoubtedly true, what it fails to account for is the market manipulation that occurs in all markets and all timeframes. And in order to see inside the market, and what the insiders and market makers are doing, we have one tool at our disposal which reveals their activity instantly, and that tool is volume. Volume is the catalyst which when combined with price, provides the foundation stone that is volume price analysis.

But if you think volume price analysis is a new approach, think again.

This approach was first developed by the founding father of technical analysis, Charles Dow, more than a century ago, and then further developed by one of the greatest traders of all time, Richard Wyckoff. Iconic traders such as Jesse Livermore and Richard Ney also used the same approach, and all had one thing in common. They used the ticker tape, reading the prices and associated volumes to interpret and anticipate future direction through the prism of volume and price.

And indeed as Richard Wyckoff wrote in the introduction to his own course in the 1930s ' you draw from the tape or from your charts, the comparatively few facts which you require for your purpose.' These facts are...the price movement, the intensity of trading, the relationships between price movement and volume, and the time required for all the movements to run their respective courses.

The concept of this technical approach to trading is very simple. It is based on the idea that every market is manipulated, and in accepting this fact, we can then conclude the market makers, the insiders and the big operators know where they are taking the market next. If so, then all we need to do to succeed as traders it to follow them. In other words, to buy when they buy, to sell when they sell, and to stay out when they are not participating. These are the simple concepts of this approach to technical analysis, and their participation or lack of participation is all revealed through the prism of price and volume, and what we call volume price analysis.

If you are already familiar with these concepts and ideas which I explain fully in 'A Complete Guide To Volume Price Analysis' then the worked examples here will provide further insights and explanations which expand on the basic concepts. However, if these are new to you, and perhaps you have been trading the forex markets for some time, but have not applied these ideas before, let me try to provide a brief overview of the terminology and concepts of this methodology.

And the first idea is very simple in that embracing volume price analysis, we are also embracing the concept that every major market is managed by those on the inside. But before we move on, let me address one issue immediately which is the criticism leveled at using volume in the world of spot forex.

We all know there is no currently central exchange in the spot market, and as such we therefore have to turn to an alternative measure of volume, which is tick activity, and is a proxy for volume. My own view, and proven over many years, is that this volume works perfectly well, and in exactly the same way as in other markets. After all, volume is simply a measure of activity or a lack of activity, and if activity is very high or very low, then this signals participation or a lack of participation by the institutional market makers. There have also been many studies over the years which have compared tick activity with the true futures volumes, and the conclusion in every case is that proxy volume is an excellent measure and barometer of 'true' volume.

For the spot forex market the insiders here are the institutional market makers, who create the price spreads, and just like the market makers in the world of stocks, can see both sides of the market, and the balance of supply and demand. The analogy I always use is to think of them as wholesalers with a warehouse of stock which is constantly being refilled and then emptied before being restocked once again. The sole purpose of the market maker is to make money from themselves, and as they sit in the privileged position of seeing both sides of the market, this is relatively simple to achieve. After all, as they see both sides of the buy and sell equation, if they themselves are short of stock and wish to replenish their warehouse, all that's required is to create a panic move in the market, which then shakes investors out of strong positions with the market makers then gratefully stepping in to buy. And the mechanism they use to great effect is the constant stream of news that drives sentiment 24 hours a day.

And whilst the institutional market makers can hide in relatively obscurity at the centre of the market, there is one activity they cannot hide, and that is volume. As the institutional market makers are by nature large in size, their participation, or lack of participation is also very clear, as price moves on large volume signal the market makers are joining the move. Conversely large moves on low volume signal a trap, with the market makers simply moving the price, but with no participation themselves. Their involvement or lack of involvement is clearly signaled through the analysis of one indicator, which is volume, and when combined with an understanding of price, we can then interpret precisely what the market makers are doing and why. And in doing so, we have a clear picture of where the market is heading next.

This methodology was codified by Richard Wyckoff in his three laws. The third law of effort and result, the second law of cause and effect, and the first law of supply and demand.

In the third law, this states that effort and result must be in agreement. In other words the volume which is the effort, must be in agreement with the outcome of the price move, or the result. If there is high volume, then we should expect to see a significant move in the price which matches the effort. If not, then this is an anomaly, and is sending a signal that something is wrong. From this anomaly in price and volume we can then interpret whether the market makers are buying or selling at this point.

Wyckoff's second law then introduces the concept of time and enshrined in the law of cause and effect. Here the law states that if the cause is large then the effect should also be large if the two are in agreement. In other words, if the time taken to build the next phase of a campaign by the market makers is large, then we should expect to see this reflected in an extended move in the price action as a result. You can think of this as the effect of winding the spring of a clockwork toy. The more the spring is wound, the greater the energy is stored, and the greater the distance the toy will travel, once it is released. This is the basic principle of cause and effect.

Finally we come to Wyckoff's first law of supply and demand, which states simply that when supply outweighs demand, then prices will fall, and when demand outweighs supply, the prices will rise.

These three laws then combine to explain and describe the constant journey of price, which moves in an endless journey from bearish to bullish and back again in all timeframes. This journey is self similar, and follows the same pattern, whether on a 1 minute chart or a 1 month chart, and a complete cycle is defined as moving from the selling climax to the buying climax and back again. But in volume price analysis we always view volume and price from the market makers perspective, in other words from the inside out. So when we talk of a selling climax, this is when the market makers are selling at the top of a rally higher, and equally a buying climax occurs at the bottom of a move lower. This is the opposite to what traders and investors understand, and is the reason most traders sell at the buying climax and buy at a selling climax.

In the selling climax, the market or stock has been rising very strongly, and those nervous investors and traders can wait no longer. Their fear of missing out is rising constantly, and finally they are drawn in to buy at the top, just at the point the market makers are selling into an increasingly weak market. The climatic price action is then created using volatility and news, which allows the market makers to clear their warehouses in preparation for the next phase of the campaign which will be to move the price lower in due course, but only when they are ready. The emotion that is used here to trigger buying by the weak hands, is the fear of missing out, or FOMO. This is a powerful emotion, and one the market makers and insiders use to great effect.

The buying climax occurs when the market makers wish to restock their empty warehouse, and here the trigger is fear of a loss. The market is moved fast into a price waterfall, generally on news, with traders and investors then selling in panic, with the market makers then stepping in to buy, and stop the stock or market falling further. Again the climax will be characterised by volatile price action and spikes in volume. Once the buying climax is complete and the warehouses are full once more, the next phase of price action begins.

This is also the reason markets fall far more quickly than they rise. The market makers can take their time in the move higher to maximise their profits, and to take these slowly. But in the move lower, they are in a hurry to fill the warehouse and repeat the process, and you can think of this as an old fashioned game of snakes and ladders. Up the ladders slowly, and down the snakes very quickly.

I use the word campaign in many of these examples, as this is precisely how it is planned by the market makers. In other words, just like a military campaign with nothing left to chance. After all, the worst thing that can happen, once a campaign is underway, is for it to be overwhelmed with increased selling or buying, and so bringing the development of the new trend to an abrupt halt. And this is where the test becomes all important.

Once an extended phase of accumulation has come to an end, and before the campaign begins, the market makers and insiders will test in order to ensure all the selling pressure has been absorbed. This ensures the bullish trend can develop slowly and smoothly, with no chance of any lingering sellers then driving the market lower. The test is executed with a move to the downside and close near the open, and is confirmed if volume is low. What we call a test of supply, and if it is a successful test on low volume, then the campaign can be launched.

Equally at the end of a distribution phase, and prior to development of the bearish trend, a test of demand is executed. Here the market makers push the price higher, and if there is little or no demand, then the price closes back near the open on low volume. This confirms the test has been successful and the campaign can begin.

Moving on, if the primary principle for accepting volume price analysis as a valid methodology is that all markets are managed and manipulated from the inside out, the second principle then follows, in that all we are looking to achieve is to identify when the market makers are buying or selling, or simply not participating in any move. And this is done very simply by considering the price action and volume both individually and also over time, and by considering whether the two are in agreement or disagreement. If price and volume are in agreement, then all is well and the market makers are driving the move and participating. If not, then we have disagreement, and from which we can then draw some logical conclusions as to whether they are buying or selling, and if so to what extent, and based on the preceding price action.

And one of the most important areas on the price chart is where a market is in congestion. Markets spend 70% to 80% of their time in such regions, and the remainder of the time trending. The reason for this is very simple. Congestion zones are the areas where trends are born, and where the market makers and insiders are preparing for the next stage of a campaign. They may be major areas, such as the selling or buying climax, or they may be minor where a market has paused in the primary trend, and developed into a second trend reversal before returning to the primary trend.

Understanding congestion phases, as well as support and resistance is a key aspect of volume price analysis, and one which many traders do not understand or simply ignore in the constant search for a trend. Indeed, breakout trading is often condemned as futile and risky by those traders and investors who have not embraced volume as part of their approach. When any breakout occurs, volume will confirm whether the move is genuine or false. It is very clear and very simple.

Traditional support and resistance based on price is a core concept of volume price analysis, and in my own trading and investing, I also incorporate volume using the volume point of control which displays volume on the price axis of the chart, and so describes the volume histogram at the various price regions and price levels. This is based on the concepts of market profile where 'fair value' occurs at the highest concentration of volume on the chart, and which also introduces the concept of time to the volume, price relationship. In other words, the longer a currency pair remains at a price level, then the greater the concentration of volume, and price will only continue to move on, once the balance of bearish or bullish sentiment has changed.

I refer to this as the volume point of control because it is the fulcrum point at which a currency pair is balanced. In other words, the bullish and bearish sentiment is equally balanced. At higher and lower levels, high volume and low volume nodes are also created, and these can then be used in the same was as for price resistance and support. In other words, if a low volume node is approached in due course, then we can expect the market to move through relatively quickly as there is little in the way of transacted volume to cause a pause in price action.

In addition, if the market considered this area to be of little significance in the past, then it is unlikely to be of great significance in the present or future. Equally, if we have a high volume node then the opposite is expected, with a pause and move into congestion then likely. Using volume in this way on the Y axis of the price chart, then gives us two perspectives on support and resistance with one based on price, which is the more traditional approach, and the other based on volume using the volume point of control indicator.

And finally, just a word or two about what we mean by volume.

For stocks and ETF's, this is the volume reported through the physical exchange. For futures, it is the futures volume, and for spot forex, it is the proxy volume of tick activity. All are very different, but all report activity and volume, and if you have a price chart with volume, then you can apply this methodology to any chart and to any timeframe. But volume is always relative, both to the session and time of year. At seasonal periods we see a general decline in volume, which is to be expected. For example when markets are closed for holidays we see low volume.

Volume reveals the truth behind price action. It reveals precisely what the market makers or insiders are planning to do next. And as a trader or investor, there is really only one thing we ever want to know, namely the answer to the question of where is the market going next. And if you can answer this question with some degree of confidence, then you will take your investing and trading to a new and exciting level. But remember, there is nothing new in trading. This approach has been around for over 100 years. It has stood the test of time, and has been adopted by some of the greatest traders of the past and present.

For myself, I have used this approach for over twenty years, and for me, a chart without volume only tells half the story. And even more important, if you have an existing approach which you use currently, there is no need to change. Simply add volume price analysis to your toolkit, and I know it will help you enormously in your own forex trading.

Section One - Daily charts

In this section we start with several worked examples using the daily timeframe from the spot forex market. All the examples in this section are taken using the NinjaTrader platform.

When using the daily timeframe for any analysis, it is always important to remember two things.

First volume can and is seasonal. Second, when markets are having a public holiday, this too is reflected in the volume on the day. Typically on the daily charts we tend to see volumes decline in the summer months, then generally rise again into the final quarter, before falling once more as we come to the end of the year with many institutions closing out their books early in December, with volume remaining low until the second week in January.

The second issue is public holidays, and it is very easy to forget this when scanning a daily chart, with low volume bars then being misinterpreted.

Worked Examples

AUD/CAD - daily - Oct to Dec 2017

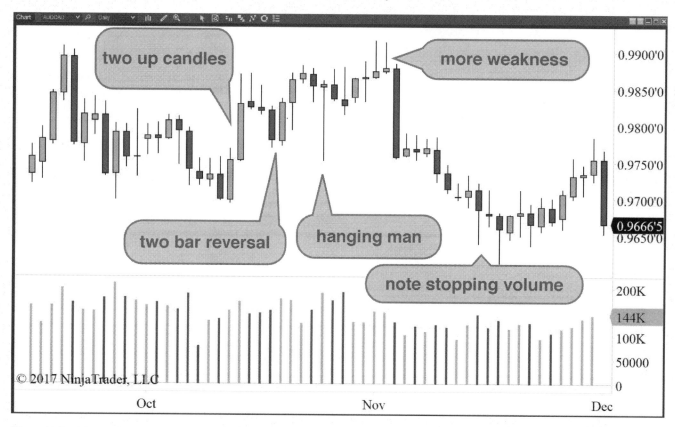

The daily chart is always an excellent place to start, whether for a longer term perspective of the pair, or simply to consider the previous day's price action which can provide some clues from an intraday perspective. So in the first group of examples, we are going to start with the daily chart, and all of these were taken towards the end of 2017 over a 60 day period, and starting with the AUD/CAD.

As always, there are many lessons we can learn here and the starting point is as the price action develops, moving deeper into October with the two up candles. And the first point to note with both these candles is the volume. Compare the volume on both with the highest volume of the month up to that point, which was in late September.

The volume for both candles looks average, and not perhaps what we should expect, particularly on the second candle which has seen a dramatic move higher, but the volume here is only marginally higher than the previous candle. This looks to be an anomaly, and an early warning signal the market makers are not participating here, but simply moving prices higher in preparation for a new campaign. From a price perspective the second candle is also signaling some weakness given the depth of the wick to the upper body, so we have two signals here.

This initial weakness is confirmed over the following two days, with two shooting star candles, but again the volume is only average here, so suggesting we are not yet ready for a bigger move. And whilst the pair does fall the following day we have a two bar reversal with the pair attempting to rally higher, but note the fall in volume.

The pair is attempting to rise, but on falling volume, giving us a further signal of potential weakness ahead. This is then followed by a series of candles signaling we are approaching a top, and that we should be prepared for a move lower, and a new campaign to start.

First comes the hanging man candle, the first sign of heavy selling but the market makers are not ready yet and the pair is supported on high volume. The hanging man candle is always one to look out for at the top of a rally as it is the first sign of selling entering the market following a move higher. What is happening here is the market is weak, and staring to sell, but the market makers move in to buy the selling as they are not yet ready to develop the new campaign.

The hanging man alone is not sufficient to provide a strong signal, but when it is followed by subsequent signals of weakness, then its significance is increased, as is the case here, as it is followed by three further shooting star candles. The first of these comes two days later on very high volume, with the final two on good volume, adding further weight. Now it is not a question of if this pair will develop into the new bearish trend, but when, and the following day the wide spread down candle signals the start of the new campaign.

This develops into mid November before stopping volume arrives and further 'mopping up' follows, before the rally higher develops off the lows on rising volume. However the penultimate candle signals further weakness. The price action is rising with volume, but the pair is struggling as signaled with the wick to the upper body of this candle. More effort is being exerted by the market makers but the market is unresponsive to higher prices, so the price action reflects this fact.

On the 1st of December, the pair duly roll over, and pick up the bearish momentum once again, and if the floor of 0.9650 is breached then we can expect to see a deeper move lower in due course.

AUD/CHF - daily - Oct to Dec 2017

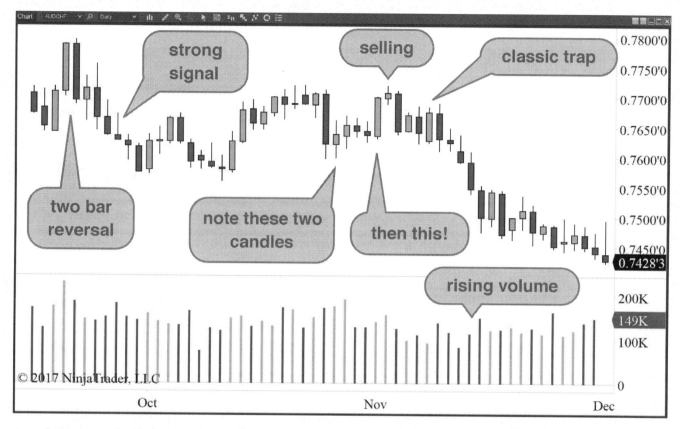

Another example from an Aussie dollar cross pair, this time for the AUD/CHF. The starting point here is to the left of the chart with the two bar reversal, which is often a strong signal, and one that is easy to spot as it is easy to overlay one candle with another to create what would be a shooting star candle on a two day chart.

This is one of the easiest 'multiple candle' patterns to view quickly and without reference to the appropriate chart, and we have several examples here, which was one reason I selected this as an example. This is the first.

The bearish trend duly develops, and then we see a strong signal this trend is set to continue with the weak attempt to rally during the day on high volume, with the candle closing with a deep wick to the upper body.

This is a classic candle, and associated volume profile to watch out for in any move lower because it signals further weakness to come. The market makers are selling here into an already weakened market, hoping to draw in traders who are buying on dips on the expectation the move is over.

It is not, as we can see clearly from the volume associated with the candle. Clearly the market makers are selling, and selling heavily, so we expect further downside price action, which arrives over the next two days.

The pair then move into an extended congestion phase, and in a tight range during the course of which we see several strong signals, along with some classic traps set by the market makers.

If we start towards the end of October, and note the two candles that follow the down candle.

Here we have rising volume which is high on both, yet the price spread on the day is very narrow, sending a strong signal the market makers are selling heavily into a weak market. After all, on such high volume we should expect to see a wide spread up candle on both with a significant rise in price action. We have neither, and only a marginal move higher.

Three candles later we then see a wide spread up candle on the day, but look at the volume. It is only average and substantially lower than our previous two candles. This is a classic trap being set by the market makers moving the price higher whilst not participating themselves.

The following day they sell, with the narrow spread candle on rising volume telling its own story. The market makers are selling into weakness here and preparing for the campaign to develop.

The wide spread down candle then creates the evening star pattern of a top with the two bar reversal of early November then firing the starting gun with the bearish trend developing on rising volume and down we go.

Note the weak attempt to rally on falling volume before the bearish trend is resumed and further confirmed over the last three candles on the chart with volume and price confirming further weakness ahead for the pair.

AUD/JPY - daily- Oct to Dec 2017

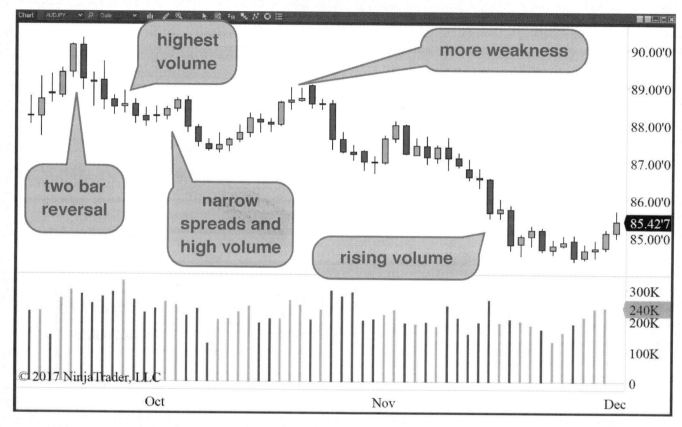

Some more great lessons on the daily chart this time on the AUD/JPY, and in particular the signals which will help to provide very strong signs of a continuation of the primary bearish trend.

Joining a trend once established can be extremely difficult, but not when applying volume price analysis, which is one of the most powerful applications of this methodology as the signals are clear and unequivocal.

If we begin with the two bar reversal to the left of the chart, this is then followed immediately with the hanging man before the bearish sentiment then starts to develop, and three candles later we see the highest volume of the session, and associated with a strong signal of weakness to come, with the wick to the upper body of a narrow spread candle.

This is followed a few days later with further confirming signals, as the pair rallies over two days, but on narrow spread candles and high volume. Here the market makers are selling into weakness, hence the reason the price action is narrow.

This is the equivalent of driving a car up a steep hill on an icy road. As the road becomes steeper more pressure is applied to the accelerator, but the car will eventually slow and perhaps reach a point at which it is stationary, with the wheels spinning and failing to grip. It is the same here. Effort and result are in disagreement giving us a clear anomaly, and perfect example of Wyckoff's third law.

Bearish momentum develops with the pair move into congestion and a rally, before we see a further example of weakness with the two shooting star candles on high volume. Again a classic example of weakness as the market makers sell.

At this point bearish momentum then picks up pace, with the classic rising volume and falling price confirming this in mid November as the 87.00 price handle is breached and potential support broken.

What is interesting now is the slowing of the bearish trend as we move to the right of the chart, and into early December.

Here we can see the bearish volumes falling, and price action is starting to flatten off. In the final few candles bullish momentum is now developing on rising volume, and with a solid platform of support now in place looks set to test resistance in the 87.00 area in the short term.

AUD/NZD - daily- Oct to Dec 2017

I selected this example for two reasons. First to highlight the comparative nature of volume and price, and second to illustrate a powerful example of the tricks the market makers play.

The candle to focus on here is the wide spread up candle of mid October.

Imagine the number of traders jumping into this move on the expectation of the development of bullish momentum, only to be left stranded, anxious and increasingly fearful as the pair promptly reverses a few days later, leaving them in a weak position, and no doubt closing out at a loss or being stopped out in due course.

The key here is the associated volume and the first question to ask is always:- Does this look right?

And the answer, of course, is no. For such a powerful move, and according to Wyckoff's third law, this type of result should be matched with an equivalent amount of effort, and clearly this is not the case.

And for comparison we would only have had to look to the left of the chart (the right would not have been created at this point) to look for equivalent volume bars and their associated price action. And the instant conclusion is clear.

This is a trap. The volume should be double or more for such a dramatic move, so clearly the market makers are not participating and instead setting a trap for the unwary.

And indeed the following day also makes the point. Here we have an almost equivalent amount of volume, but look at the price action, it is very contained.

This confirms two things. First we are correct in thinking this is a trap, and second the pair is being set up for a bearish trend.

Further signals of weakness then follow over the next few days with the two bar reversal, and shooting star candles all adding to this view with the pair reversing and moving lower into the bearish trend.

AUD/USD - daily - Oct to Dec 2017

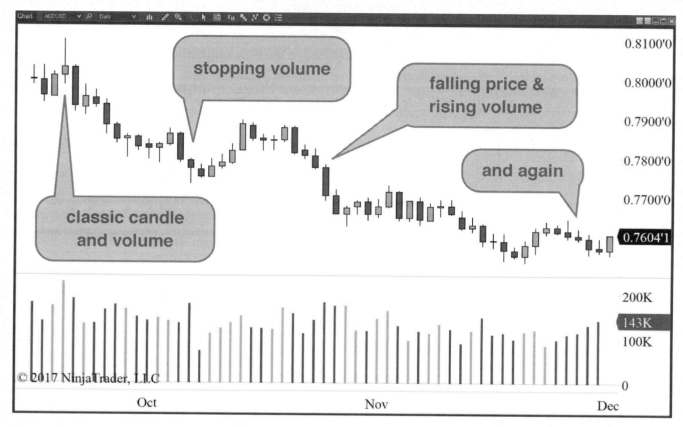

Finally for the Aussie dollar we come to the major for the currency against the US dollar, and some excellent examples of volume price analysis in action in the longer term bearish trend.

We start here with the fourth candle from the left of the chart, and also the highest volume of the period, and a classic combination of the shooting star candle and ultra high volume.

In this case the reaction is instant with a wide spread down candle the following day.

This happens, but is not always the case, and it is easy to jump into the market on such a strong signal of weakness.

Such immediate reversals do happen, but it is more common for the market to congest first before changing direction from one campaign to another, so patience is often required.

In this case the price waterfall develops nicely before the market makers step in to buy in early October, driving the price up into a congestion phase which then breaks down in classic fashion on falling prices and rising volume, and re-establishment of the primary trend once more.

More recently, towards the end of November we have seen this pattern repeated in less dramatic style, but with no signs just yet of stopping volume, the bearish trend looks set to continue for the medium term.

CAD/JPY - daily - Oct to Dec 2017

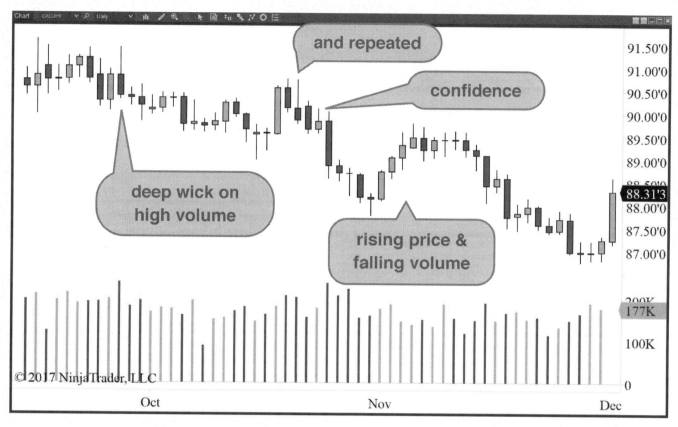

The CAD/JPY daily chart is yet another which delivers some excellent lessons on reading the re-establishment of the primary trend following a move into a secondary trend in the move lower.

Once again we start to the left of the chart in mid September. Here we have a classic congestion phase building, with signs of weakness that are finally confirmed with the highest volume of the session, and the deep wick candle of late September.

The bearish momentum for the pair is given a further injection of momentum in mid October with a repeat performance, and the price waterfall then developing.

Note the candle that adds further to this signal two candles later, which would have given us confidence to join the move lower at this point.

Early November then sees a rally begin, but at this point we cannot be sure whether this is a reversal of the primary trend into a bullish trend higher, or simply a secondary trend - in other words a pullback before the primary trend is re-established.

However, note the volume and price action which is a tell tale sign. Rising prices and falling volume, and moreover on narrowing spreads. This looks weak for sure, and is most certainly only a temporary reversal.

In other words, a secondary trend within the primary, which is then re-established in mid November.

Finally note the candles and volume of late November. Here we see high volume and narrow spread candles signaling the market makers are moving in to buy, and it is no surprise to see the rally higher on the last to candles of the chart.

EUR/CHF - daily - Oct to Dec 2017

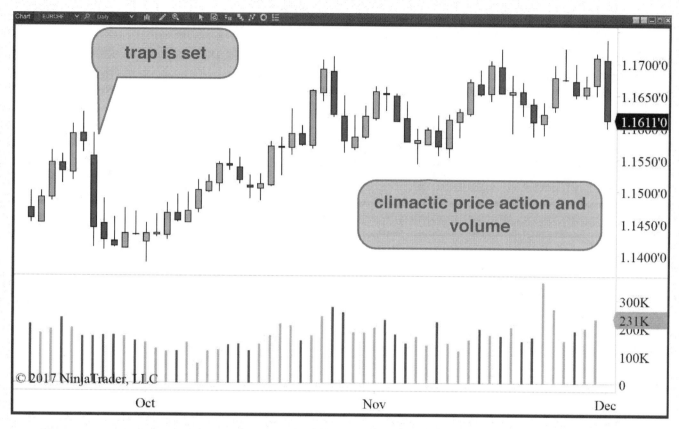

As we move to some of the euro pairs, this is a great example of the tricks the market makers frequently play, moving price dramatically in one direction, but with no participation from themselves. Traders are then left trapped in weak positions as the market reverses.

In this case, the trap move was to the downside, and clearly apparent with the wide spread down candle on average volume of late September.

Indeed for comparison we would only have had to look at the high volume of earlier in the month to gain some idea of whether this was high medium or low volume.

What is clear, is the market makers are not participating here, so a trap is being set, which is duly sprung for the remainder of October as the pair rally strongly.

Traders who jumped in on the expectation of some easy and quick profits are left stranded, and no doubt stopped out or have to close out at a loss.

27

What then develops from late October onwards, and through to the early December is classic climactic price action, as the pair moves into a period of consolidation, which is characterised with volatile moves and spikes in volume, both low and high.

In addition, and as part of the climax, a strong ceiling of resistance is also being built in the 1.1700 region with constant tests, and retests, all of which fail to break through this key level, and with a triple top now in development, this pair is looking increasingly bearish in this timeframe.

The floor of support is equally important with a move through 1.1550 then opening the way to a sustained bearish trend developing in the medium term.

EUR/GBP - daily - Oct to Dec 2017

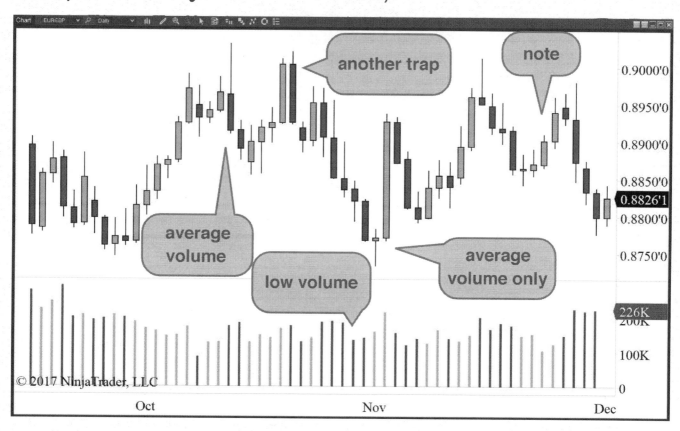

I selected this example on the EUR/GBP pair for several reasons, and not least to provide a 'close up' view of the selling climax, and in particular the volatile type of price action we expect to see in such phases.

Both the selling climax and the buying climax are characterised with whipsaw price action that changes direction often and violently, and is associated with volume both high and low. What happens in these phases is very simple.

The market makers are moving price rapidly from bearish to bullish and back again, to constantly draw traders who then become trapped in weak positions.

For example, traders who are fearful of missing out on the move higher, buy and are then caught when the market reverses lower, where traders who are looking to sell, jump in.

The market then reverses higher again, where those traders who were long exit, grateful to have taken just a small loss.

The market then reverses again, and those traders who were short do the same thing and exit. It is a constant process of push and pull. The market makers' objective in all of this is to sell prior to a campaign lower, and in amongst all this price action, the traps are many and varied.

In October we can see several.

The dramatic candle with the deep wick, and only average volume. The two bar reversal, which again is on average volume, and finally the move lower towards the end of the month on low volume. November then opens with another, a wide spread up candle on average volume. Clearly no participation here by the market makers, with the pair promptly reversing over the following days.

This is followed by a rapid move higher, but note the volume it is average at best, with the top then created and rolling over. This trick is repeated again on even lower volume this time, before turning lower almost instantly.

All clever tricks, and all clearly signaling the market makers are not joining in here and merely pushing the market this way and that in the selling climax. At some point heavy selling will ensue, and then the next campaign will begin in earnest.

EUR/NZD - daily - Oct to Dec 2017

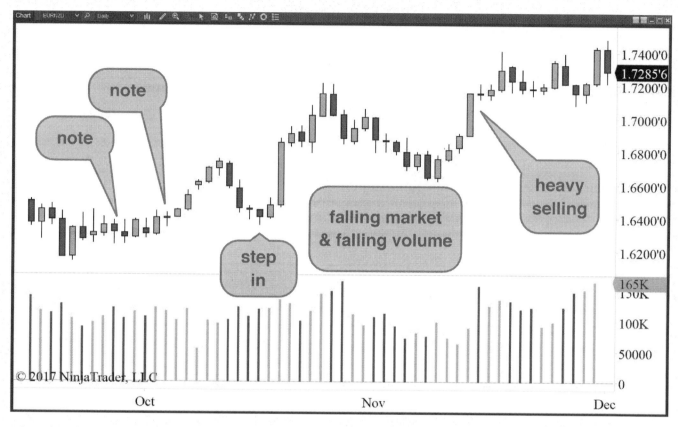

This is an interesting chart, where we start on the left in September with a congestion phase as the market makers accumulate, and prepare for the next phase of the campaign.

Note the buying in late September and early October with the rally duly launched. However, by mid October this has run out of steam and selling ensues, but the market makers step in very quickly on the two narrow spread down candles to buy, thereby driving the pair higher once more.

The two bar reversal then arrives at the top of the rally, and bearish sentiment then takes hold.

However, note the general decline in the volume under each subsequent down candle. Here we have a falling market, but the selling volumes are also declining and sending a clear signal this reversal lacks strength and is unlikely to go far.

The two bar reversal signals the bottom, and the pair rally higher again, but note the volume on the wide spread up candle.

It is only average, and a warning signal the market makers are not helping to drive this market higher. Then we see the reason why on the next candle. Ultra high volume and a narrow spread candle.

The market makers are now selling heavily into weakness here, and this is further confirmed with the following three candles.

Two narrow spread candles on high volume followed by a third with a deep wick, and again on high volume.

And moving to the extreme right of the chart, now we can see ultra high volumes building with two further two bar reversals to the up side in the final two weeks.

This chart is now developing into a top, with high and rising volume failing to drive the market higher.

EUR/USD - daily - Oct to Dec 2017

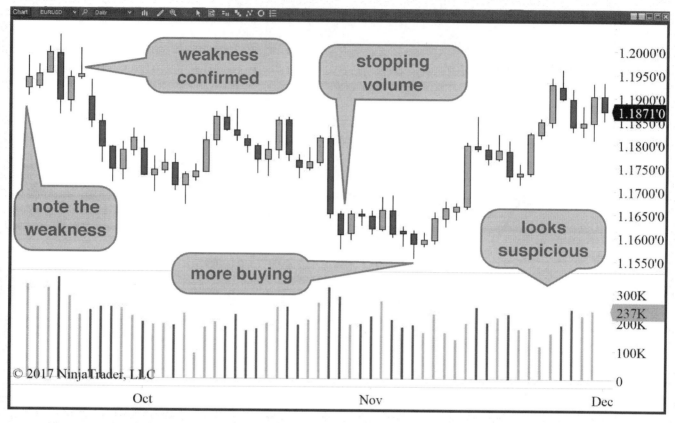

The euro dollar is every scalper's favourite pair, and yet with some attention to the daily chart, may help to provide context and confidence for the day and days ahead.

The first point of note is the very first candle. Extreme volume and a very weak candle, with further very high volume driven into two relatively narrow spread candles, suggesting weakness ahead.

This appears the following day and is further confirmed two days later with the shooting star candle on falling volume. The gapped down bearish candle then starts the run of three days of down candles on good volume.

The next area of the chart is towards the end of October.

First we have the wide spread down candle, and followed the next day by stopping volume and buying by the market makers.

Further buying then follows in the mopping up phase, and the pair rallies before delivering a shooting star candle on high volume with a consequent reversal lower.

Finally note the sudden sharp rally of late November on average to low volume.

This looks very suspicious, so it is no surprise to see the pair move into a congestion phase with no follow through. The market makers here are not participating, and simply moving the price higher before selling into the reversal.

In addition, the price action is now approaching an area of resistance to the left of the chart, so we can expect further consolidation in this region.

GBP/CHF - daily - Oct to Dec 2017

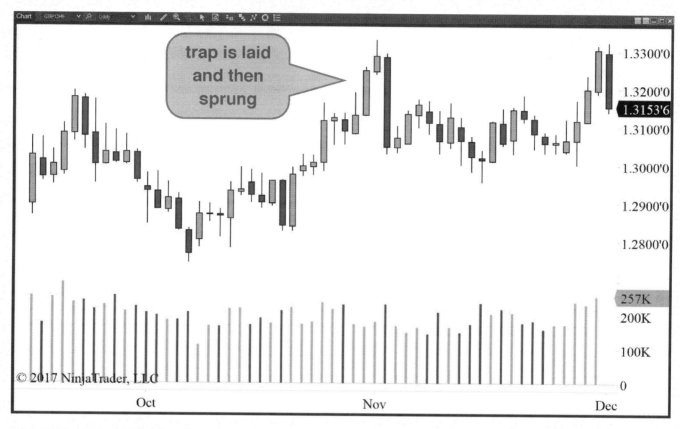

This is another chart that has many lessons, but the one I want to focus on particularly, is once again an example where understanding when the market makers are not participating in a move is just as important as understanding when they are.

The price action of note here develops in the centre of the chart at the very end of October, and the start of November.

And the key thing to remember here is the price action to the left will already be available for benchmarking this region in terms of the associated volume.

So if we start with the first of the three up candles. This looks weak, and had we looked at this set up at the end of the day, our expectation would be to see some weakness to follow.

But this is not the case, and the pair rallies strongly the following day, albeit on slightly lower volume.

This now looks very odd, and for comparison and a benchmark, we only have to find an equivalent candle in terms of spread, and consider the volume, to appreciate this is indeed a trap move, and one which is likely to come to an abrupt end.

The price action then continues higher for a third day, but again looks weak, as there is a wick to the upper body of the candle, on the same average volume.

This makes the previous day's price action even more suspicious, and the warning bells are now ringing loud and clear.

The following day bullish traders are trapped as the pair falls dramatically. The trap was laid and then sprung.

GBP/JPY - daily - Oct to Dec 2017

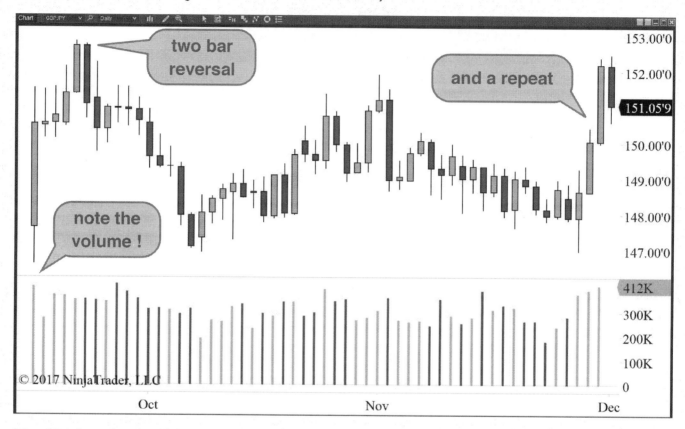

The GBP/JPY is one of the most volatile of all the principle currency pairs, and its nickname of 'the dragon' is one that is well deserved, as moves of over 200 pips in the day are relatively common.

The term I use to describe price action in this pair is the 'soufflé effect' which is price action that rises quickly, but collapses equally as fast. And we have the perfect example here as we start to the left of the chart.

The first candle is dramatic by any standards, with a range of over 400 pips on the day. But note the volume, which by any 'common sense' standard should be dramatic when associated with such a move.

But the volume is not dramatic, and we simply see volume that is high, but not excessively so.

This should set the alarm bells ringing immediately as it is clearly an anomaly under Wyckoff's third law of effort and result.

The result here is huge, but the effort is average. The two aspects are in disagreement and therefore an alarm bell sounds.

But we're not done just yet, and over the following few days, we see further signs of weakness which merely confirm what we first thought, and in addition add weight to the fact that a trap has been laid once again.

After all, the volume bars over the following days is of the same height as on the first candle, so this must be a false move. The market makers are planning a campaign here and not participating.

Then the two bar reversal arrives, and the trend lower begins and gathers momentum.

However, note the volume which is generally falling with the falling market, so whilst we have strong bearish momentum, we do not expect this to continue into a sustained rout given the selling pressure which is declining.

And the trap described here is then repeated on the last four candles of the chart. A rapid and sustained move on three candles of equal volume, before coming to a shuddering halt on the first day of December.

GBP/USD - daily - Oct to Dec 2017

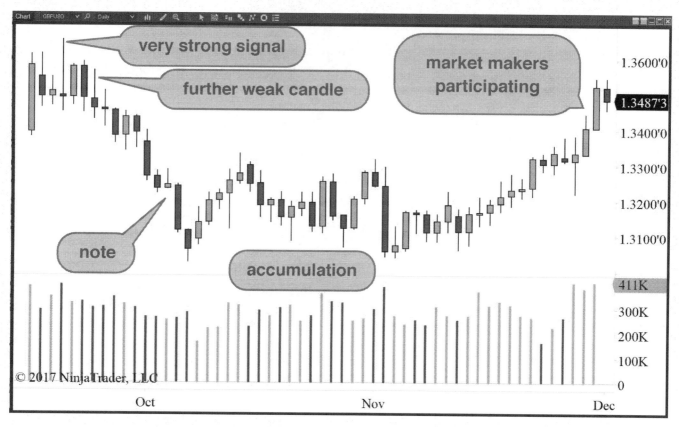

This chart for cable could best be described as a game of two halves, with the selling climax to the left, the price waterfall, and subsequent buying climax and accumulation in the middle, before the reversal in primary trend and rally to the right.

If we start on the left, the first very strong signal is on the deep wick shooting star candle, coupled with very high volume and a clear signal the market makers are selling heavily here.

This is followed by the two bar reversal which confirms the weakness, and is followed by a further weak candle closing with a deep wick to the upper body and high volume once again.

The price waterfall then develops accordingly. Note the candle which precedes the second leg down, and is a strong entry point for those who missed the initial bearish signal.

Then we move into the accumulation phase with the pair trading in a range of 200 pips with insider buying apparent and weak rallies, before the move higher finally gathers momentum in the final few days of November on high volume.

Clearly the market makers are participating here and driving the pair higher, and given the strong platform of support now in place below, any move through the 1.3600 region is likely to see this trend develop further, provided the market makers continue to remain involved on supportive volume.

NZD/CAD - daily - Oct to Dec 2017

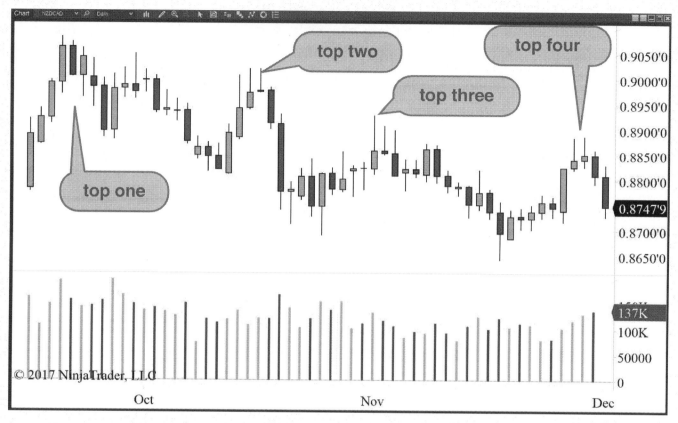

This is a great chart with four wonderful little tops formed all offering clear trading opportunities to the short side.

But what is also interesting here is that whilst the tone is bearish overall, it is not rampaging lower, but sliding lower, with each rally reaching a top that is lower than the previous, and more reminiscent of the rounded tops of a move in a bullish trend.

Nevertheless, there are plenty of clear signals here.

Top one starts with the two bar reversal lower, and is followed shortly after by a two bar reversal higher.

Then come the signals confirming weakness. Look at the volume on the candle following the wide spread up candle.

It is almost the same volume, but the price action is so weak. This is followed by lower volume on yet another weak shooting star candle. The weakness develops, and we move into the price waterfall.

Then we see the rally to top number two.

But look at the three candles leading to the shooting star candle at the top of the hill.

Both have deep wicks to the upper body, and both have good volume, and so the pair rolls over delivering two down days of price action.

Rally three then follows, but once again topped off with candles with deep wicks and good volume. A two bar reversal then adds further confirmation as the pair picks up bearish momentum.

Finally we have rally number four. And again it is a similar pattern topped off with two shooting star candles on good volume.

And down goes the pair once more.

NZD/JPY - daily - Oct to Dec 2017

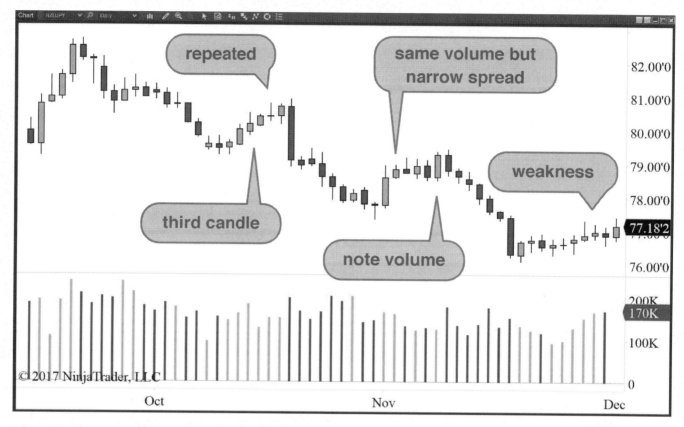

I have included this chart to show one particular aspect of volume price analysis, which is perhaps even more powerful than the entry and the exit of any position.

And that's in the ability of volume price analysis to give you confidence to hold a position in the market during the constant pullbacks and reversals, that are all part of the longer term trend.

Here we have an example of the primary trend lower, which is constantly punctuated with secondary trends as described by Wyckoff, which is the reversal against the primary trend in the timescale under consideration.

Suppose we have entered a short position, which has developed in the first move lower, but now we start to see the reversal against us as the secondary trend takes hold.

But, is this a reversal to a primary trend in the opposite direction? In other words, the development of a bullish trend higher, or simply a pullback in the move lower? How do we know, and how can we be sure? And the answer lies in applying volume price analysis.

In the first reversal what do we see?

And it is the third up candle which gives us a very strong clue.

Here we see rising volume over the first three candles, but on the third, we have a weak candle, and in addition higher volume than on the previous candle. The market makers are selling into weakness here, and this is repeated two candles later as the resistance above is tested.

So we are expecting the primary trend to be re-established, which proves to be the case, with the wide spread down candle driving momentum back into the primary trend, and on down to the next pause point.

Here we see a slightly different type of rally, but nonetheless one that should give us confidence.

After the first up candle, the next arrives on identical volume but note the spread. It is very narrow and sending a clear signal of weakness. After all, on the same volume with the preceding candle we had a wide spread up candle.

Yet here we have a narrow spread. The conclusion here is simple. The market makers are selling into weakness once again. This sequence ends with the two bar reversal but note the volume on the up candle, it is very low. And so down we go once again into the next phase of downwards momentum.

And as we move to the end of November, the same pattern of price and volume is being repeated, with volume which is rising rapidly but with no equivalent increase in price. So the bearish picture for this pair looks set to continue for the time being.

NZD/USD - daily - Oct to Dec 2017

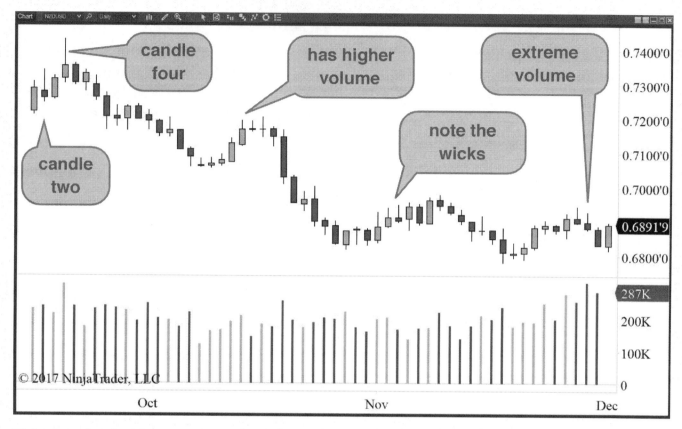

This chart for the NZD/USD has many similarities to the previous chart, and I have added it just for completeness.

Here again we have the primary bearish trend over the period punctuated with secondary trend reversals. And we start here with two very strong entry signals which appear as candles two and four on the chart starting from the left.

Candle two gives us an early warning of weakness to come on high volume with a deep wick to the upper body, candle four then confirms this signal loud and clear with an even stronger signal on extreme volume, and a very deep wick to the upper body. If we were not ready on the first signal, we should certainly be ready on the second. The price waterfall duly develops.

Then the secondary trend begins but note the price action.

We have rising volume here, but the second up candle in the sequence has higher volume than the previous candle, but the spread is narrower.

In addition, a wick has developed to the upper body. This is signaling weakness, which is confirmed two candles later with the doji.

Down we go again on rising volume before the next reversal arrives. But almost immediately weakness is signaled with the upper wicks to all these candles on good volume before the primary trend is re-established once again.

Finally note the price and volume of the last few candles in November, and in particular the extreme volume on the narrow body candles with the wicks. Two such examples one after the other. A strong signal the pair remain weak.

USD/NOK - daily - Oct to Dec 2017

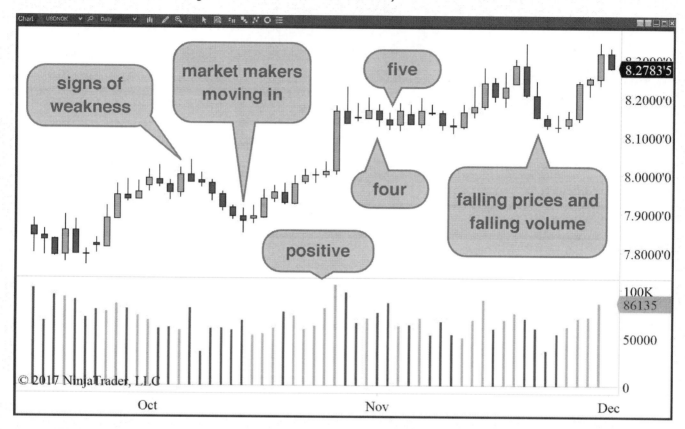

So far we have looked at a couple of examples where volume price analysis can help us to stay in a primary trend lower, and in this example for the USD/NOK we take a look at the opposite, which is holding in a primary trend higher.

The USD/NOK is one of those pairs that is increasingly available on many platforms, and with its relationship to oil, offers excellent trading opportunities in much the same way as the Canadian dollar pairs.

If we start to the left of the chart, the first rally gets underway but almost immediately starts to look rather weak as we enter October. First note the generally falling volume on the up candles in the move.

Then as we reach the top of the rally we see some signs of weakness developing, first on lower volume, but also on one high volume candle with the deep wick to the upper body confirming this weakness.

Five down days then follow, but the volume remains flat, and is not rising. Moreover, on the final candle, the spread is narrow on higher volume, signaling the market makers are now moving in to buy and support the primary trend.

The next three up candles are a positive sign on rising volume and then we see the injection of volume with the move completed with the nice wide spread up candle on the highest volume of the chart. The market makers are in full control and participating strongly.

The congestion phase then follows. The first candle in this sequence looks weak, as does the second, but then note candles four and five.

The market makers are buying here. The spreads are narrow and the volume is rising and high. If they were selling, then the spreads would be wide and down. They are not. So this must be buying to support the rally once again. Then we are off again and moving higher once more.

A top is then formed with the first down candle and wick to the upper body, but note the volume. It is smaller than many of the previous volume bars, and on the following day, lower still, with the third down day on a narrow spread, associated with the smallest volume of all. This is a classic signal, and one which gives a huge boost in confidence.

After all, if this were sustained market maker selling, then the pair would have fallen hard and fast. A falling market with rising volume is a clear signal of continuation.

Equally, and as we have here, a falling market with falling volume is a clear signal of an anomaly, and tells us the trend lower is unlikely to develop. In other words, this is simply a secondary trend reversal against the primary trend.

And so it proves to be, with the final few candles rising strongly on rising volume, and confirming the re-establishment of the primary trend higher.

USD/CAD - daily - Oct to Dec 2017

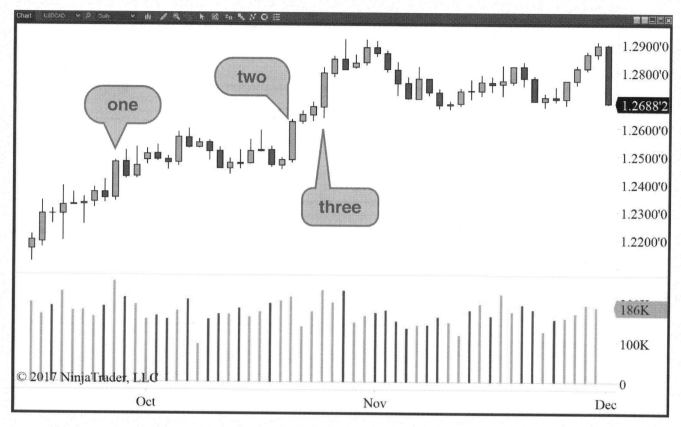

And speaking of oil, we now have an example for the USD/CAD, and the lesson here, is in using the chart to help provide a comparative approach to both volume and price.

Volume is always relative, as we are constantly trying to judge whether the volume we see with the associated price action is in agreement or disagreement.

In this context the focus is on the up candles in this move, and the most important concept here is to remember we need to compare like with like, apples with apples, and not apples wit pears.

So when comparing price action and associated volume we must try to consider like for like candles, which then provide a valid basis for comparison.

So in this example, we can compare the various wide spread up candles, of which we have three, all of similar price spread, with very small or no wicks top and bottom.

And note the volume on each - they are generally in agreement in the move higher.

Perhaps candle one is a little taller, but candles two and three look to be much the same.

This is an exercise we do all the time when studying a price chart, but when doing so, make sure to compare like for like candles in order to arrive at a valid analysis.

USD/CHF - daily - Oct to Dec 2017

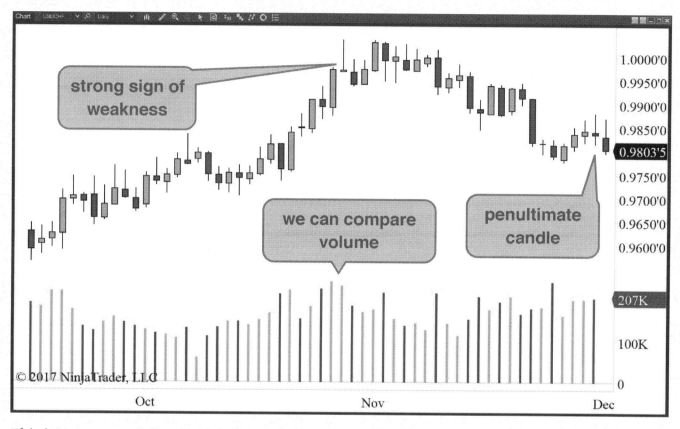

This is a very neat example of the comparative nature of volume price analysis, and here we are in a trend higher. This chart also highlights the comparison of one volume bar with another, and what this is telling us about the weakness or strength of insider buying or selling.

If we start at the centre of the chart, towards the end of October we see a strong sign of weakness with the shooting star candle on very high volume.

What is interesting here is then to compare the volume with the previous day where we saw a strong move on the day with a wide spread up candle so the market markets are buying into the move higher.

But, the following day we see a strong signal they are now selling into weakness with the same enthusiasm. And there could be several reasons for such a change in sentiment, and these include: an item of fundamental news, a change from risk on to risk off, or simply stop hunting.

However, we are not comparing the price here, only the volume which tells us this is very strong selling by the market makers. And this is further confirmed by considering other shooting star type candles in the move higher, which have much lower volume, which only resulted in minor pullbacks in the primary trend higher.

This then is a significant candle, and by comparing it with the penultimate candle on the chart, it gives us a strong sign this candle too is a strong signal of further weakness. Yes the volume is lower than our 'benchmark' shooting star at the top, but nevertheless volume here is significant, and indeed the final day reflected this bearish picture.

Once again we are comparing similar candles and on this chart we have several candles which closed with an upper wick and and narrow body.

Those in the early part of the trend higher, have relatively low volume, suggesting a lack of selling pressure and indicative of minor moves lower whilst those in the latter part of the trend higher, and into the reversal, show generally higher volume.

Comparing one with another gives us, not only great insight into the candle itself and also the context of where it is in the trend, but also whether we are simply seeing some weakness develop, or a more pronounced reversal in trend.

USD/JPY - daily - Oct to Dec 2017

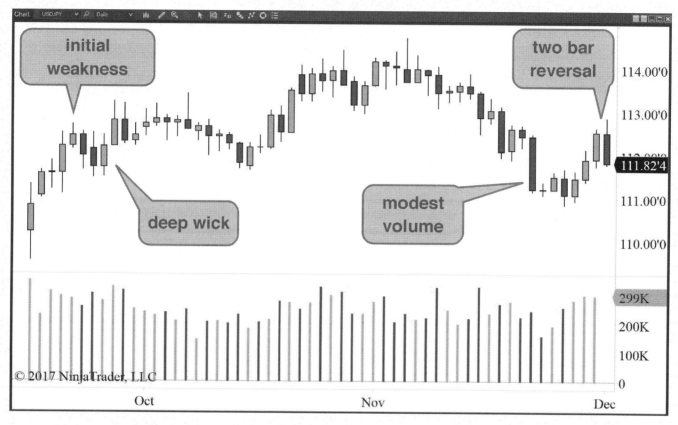

The USD/JPY is one of the trickiest pairs to trade, with many forex traders believing it follows the same pattern as other yen based pairs, or perhaps simply follows other majors driven by the US dollar.

This is most certainly not the case as the USD/JPY is a pair of risk, as the pair has risk based currencies on both sides. So this is even more of a reason to apply a methodology such as volume price analysis to help make sense of this complicated and complex pair.

And if we begin with the initial rally higher in September to the left of the chart, initial weakness becomes evident on the fifth candle in the sequence, which has the same volume as the preceding candle, but a much reduced spread on the body of the candle. Clearly the market makers are finding it hard work here and selling into weakness.

The pair attempts to rally, but on the second candle, we have a deep wick to the upper body and increased volume, which confirms the earlier signal.

The pair is looking weak, and this is confirmed several times as we move into early October before the pair move lower into the middle of the month. This move comes to an end on the two bar reversal, and the rally higher begins, but almost immediately runs into trouble, and an extended congestion phase begins, punctuated by deep wicks to the top of the candles, hanging men candles, and doji candles.

The weakness is finally triggered in mid November, but note the volume in the move lower - it is generally falling, and the final wide spread down candle has only modest volume, with the move then coming to a halt as the market makers move in and buy to take the pair higher once more.

However, given the final candle on the chart, this rally looks to have run out of steam with the two bar reversal now in place.

Section Two - Hourly charts

In this section we move from the daily timeframe to the hourly timeframe, and all the examples here are taken from the MT4 platform and once again all are for spot forex currency pairs.

The issue when considering volume in this timeframe, is to ensure we are comparing like with like as volume in one session will be very different to volume in another. For example volume in the London and US session will be much deeper than volume in the Far East and Asia session. This is something we have to be aware of as volume traders in this, or indeed any other market where volume will vary accordingly.

When comparing volume here, we can compare on two levels. First with like volume within the session itself, and then with like volume in a previous session. So here we can compare London on the day with London on a previous day, or volume in the US session with volume in a previous US session. Equally, we can compare volume in the Far East and Asia with volume in a session in history.

What we cannot compare is volume in one session with volume in another. The comparison of London volumes with Asia and Far East volumes does not reveal anything in terms of volume price analysis, other than the fact there is a huge variation - which we know anyway.

As you will see in these examples I refer to sessions, as session one, session two etc. This simply means the complete session from the London open on one day to the London open on the next. In other words, a complete 24 hour cycle.

Each of the charts that follows has five cycles, in other words is over a week of price action, and each session is characterised by the typical rise and fall in volume in the 24 hour period which creates the 'wave patterns'. To help make this easier, I have labelled each chart with a 1,2,3,4,5 notation to make this clear, and so make identifying the session referenced easier to spot.

Worked Examples

AUD/CAD - 60 minute chart

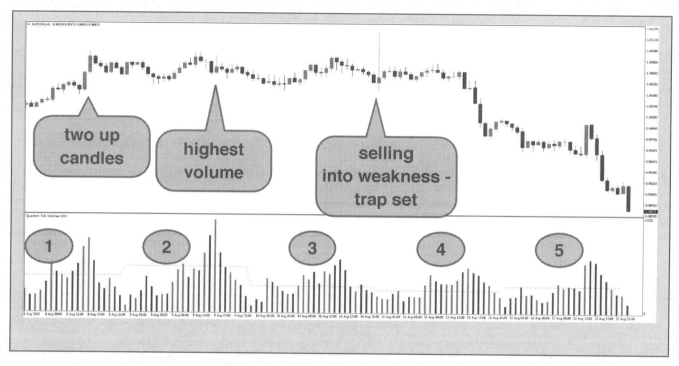

In this section we move to consider examples form the faster timeframes starting with the 60 minute chart which is one of the most popular. As before these are all taken from the spot forex world

When considering charts over the slower timeframes, there will always be a rise and fall as the session moves from deep liquidity in Europe, London and the US, into thinner volumes in Asia and the Far East. This does not invalidate any analysis, and indeed provides a benchmark session by session.

I selected this example for a particular reason and that's to show the time a pair can remain in a congestion phase, and even when we see strong volume price analysis signals, patience is always required.

Remember, markets spend far more time in congestion than they do in trend, and to take advantage of any trend, we just have to wait for the congestion phase to end.

If we start to the left of the chart, the pair rise initially with two up candles on high volume, but then move into congestion for the first session.

In the second session the highest volume is under the shooting star candle. Clearly the market makers are selling into weakness here. This consolidation phase continues into session three, before the ultra high shooting star candle appears, but note the volume.

This is in the Far East and Asia session and clearly this is a trap move as there is very low volume under the candle. The trap is being set.

Finally the market breaks in session four on high volume, with the pair then driven lower in session five as the week comes to an end.

AUD/CHF - 60 minute chart

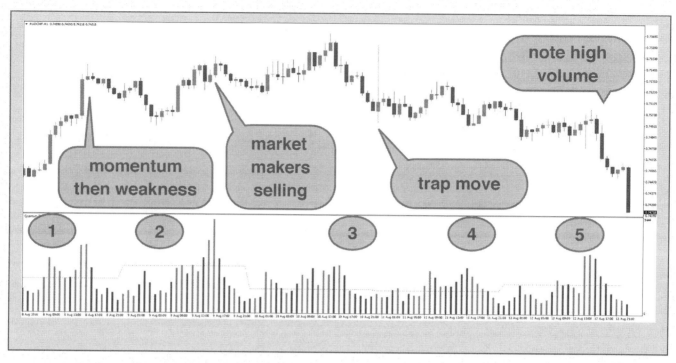

More great examples here. In the first session we see a nice steady rise for the pair with a pause, before an injection of momentum with the wide spread up candle, but immediately after we see weakness where we have the same amount of volume, but this time with a shooting star candle. This is a clear sign of weakness. The market makers are selling heavily here. And down the market goes overnight.

Session two sees the rally develop off the initial buying, but again is topped off with a weak candle on ultra high volume before drifting lower off the highs. The volume here is the highest on the chart, and note the spread of price action, and compare this to volumes seen in the first session and associated price spread.

On such extreme volume we should expect to see a dramatic move in price. We have not, so this sends a very loud signal the market makers are preparing to leave, and selling heavily into weakness here. As always we have to be patient and wait, but the signal is very clear.

Session three sees the volumes reduce, and gives an example of the comparative nature of volume across the sessions.

Clearly volumes in sessions one and two were dramatically higher, but the weakness has already been created in the pair with the market makers having sold out and continuing to sell into weakness.

The spiked shooting star on low volume confirms the trap once more.

The weakness then builds into session four on rising volume and ultimately into session five, and note the high volume of the last candle immediately before the start of the price waterfall.

AUD/JPY - 60 minute chart

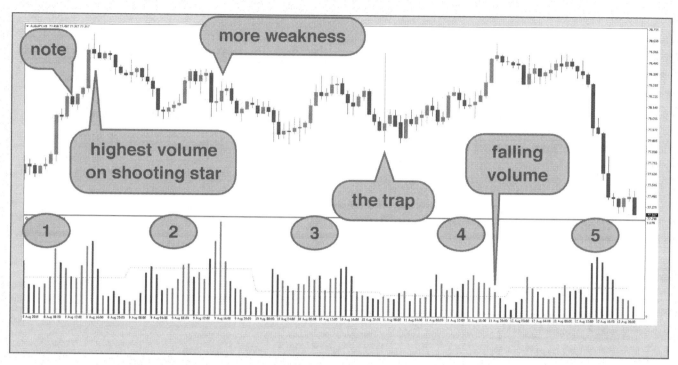

If we start to the left of the chart, the price action develops strongly, with the pair rising fast on rising volume before the top is reached with two candles.

Note the selling pressure on the second down candle in this move higher, the volume is average so sending a clear signal this move is not coming to an end just yet.

The bullish momentum continues, but then we reach the top with two candles. The first is a wide spread up candle on high volume, but note the follow up candle.

We have even higher volume, but a shooting star candle - another very clear and simple signal to see, and off we go into the Asian session with the market makers happily selling.

Session two confirms this weakness with higher volumes than in the first session failing to move the market higher, and once again confirming this weakness. Note the narrow spread of these candles and the market falls with some buying then appearing as session three begins.

However, once more weakness is confirmed and note the rally of session four on falling volume and dramatically lower than in session one.

This is looking ever weaker before finally in session five the pair collapses with sustained selling pressure in the price waterfall.

And always remember, regardless of whether you are an intraday trader or longer term trend trader, the slower timeframe charts are just as important, and can reveal so much, as well as provide a benchmark for the dominant market direction intraday.

AUD/NZD - 60 minute chart

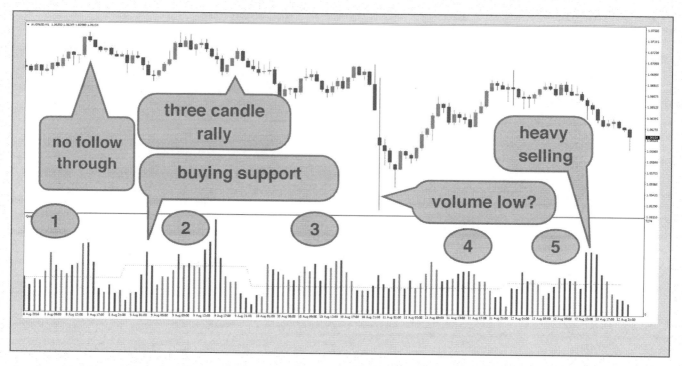

Again, another example where the focus is on the market maker selling at the top of the market rather than buying at the bottom.

If we begin on the left of the chart, intraday weakness appears with the high volume and narrow spread body on the candle. Clearly there has been no follow through from the up candle preceding it, and the remainder of the session is bearish.

The market makers are again selling into weakness here. Volume is being driven into the market as they sell, but the pair is unresponsive as the market is weak, and so all this effort appears as a narrow body on the candle. The close of the body in terms of color is not important, and may close above the open or below.

What is important is the narrow spread at the top of a rally, which signals weakness ahead, and coupled with the high volume, confirms the market makers are selling here.

Buying then appears in session two and the pair move back to test the highs, but once again weakness is signaled with the price action failing to follow through before moving lower, with high volume confirming the weakness in the down candle. The three candle rally is on falling volume, before we move into congestion in session three.

Then we see extreme volatility. But what is interesting here is the lack of volume. On such a move we should see participation.

There is none, or very little and it is impossible to predict market direction from such candles so patience is required. We have to wait for the volatility to subside and see where the market is moving once the volume has normalized.

Bullish momentum returns, before session five ends on heavy selling.

AUD/USD - 60 minute chart

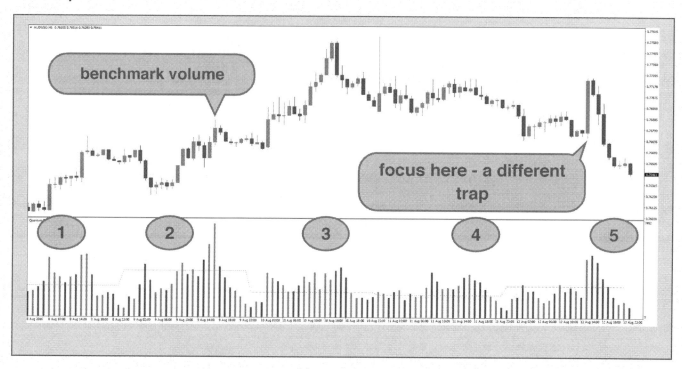

In this example let's start on the right hand side of the chart for a change, as this is the take away point from this example.

The focus here is the wide spread up candle in the final session of the period, and is a nice example with no wicks to top and bottom.

Now consider the volume, and as a benchmark consider the volume in session two, which is the highest on the chart. The price action associated with this candle was relatively narrow, and yet the candle in session five is very wide.

What can we conclude from this apparent anomaly?

Very simply, this is a trap move. Why?

Because for the market to be moved this much, and based on our benchmark volume of an earlier session, the volume should be two or three times greater. Clearly this is some sort of trap move being set by the market makers, and so it proves to be, with the pair selling off heavily for the remainder of the session.

I accept it takes courage to short after such a strong move, but volume will help to give you the confidence to take such positions in the market. Every other trader would have been jumping in long, which is precisely what the market makers want you to do.

And this also highlights how to compare volume from session to session. The volumes on a 60 minute chart will rise and fall over the twenty four hour period.

This is normal and to be expected, and reflecting the fact trading volumes in London and the US are, by definition, much higher than in Asia and the Far East, which is what we see on the chart. So in order to make sure we are comparing like volumes, we have to compare 'across the sessions'.

In other words, in the same session for a previous day. So we compare London and the US with London and the US for a previous day.

We cannot compare London and the US with Asia as we are not comparing like with like. In this example we are using the chart to signal the highest peaks in volume, which in turn gives us a benchmark for the volume we have considered in this example. And from this simple analysis, one thing is clear.

We have an anomaly of effort and result as codified in Wyckoff's third law. And from this we can deduce the market makers are not participating, but are laying a trap which is duly sprung over the next few hours.

CAD/JPY - 60 minute chart

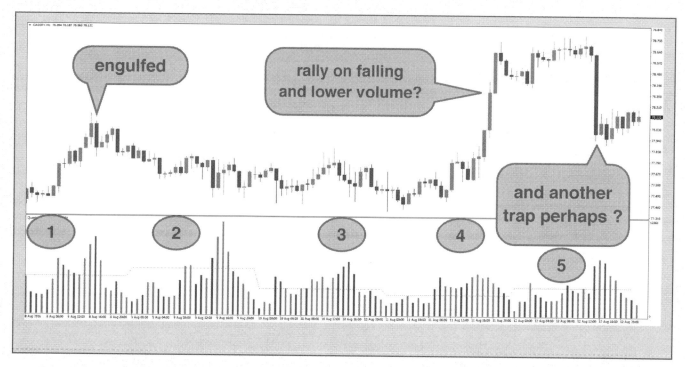

We have some tricky price action here, which would also have been heavily influenced by moves in the price of oil, as well as the weekly oil inventories, which always play a major part on an intraday basis for the Canadian dollar. So where to start?

Session one certainly has a bearish feel after the initial rally on good volume, but the final candle at the top of the rally has wicks to top and bottom, and is then engulfed by the following candle on even higher volume.

The subsequent three candle rally looks weak as we have a rising market and falling volume that really encapsulates the next few sessions. We do see buying by the market makers intraday followed by short term rallies, and then we arrive at the last two sessions and once again it is the comparative nature of volume that helps here and is the most interesting price action of the chart.

Yes, the market has rallied strongly, but look at the volume which is falling, and in addition is low when compared to volume earlier in the period, and also compared to volumes in previous same period sessions.

The alarm bell is ringing loudly here, particularly given the dramatic nature of the price action which moved vertically over a three hour period. The market makers and insiders are well aware of the emotional fear of missing out, and use it to great advantage. The market takes off, traders wait in rising panic as the the price action continues, and the fear of missing out grows exponentially.

Finally, they can wait no longer and jump in, generally just at the point the market makers have decided to reverse the trend.

The rally is then topped off with a series of doji candles before selling off with the wide spread down candle, but again, note the volume.

This looks odd on such a price move. We should expect to see ultra high volume associated with such a move, so perhaps yet another trap is being set by the institutional market makers. And indeed the down candle of two bars later confirms this fact with higher volume here.

EUR/AUD - 60 minute chart

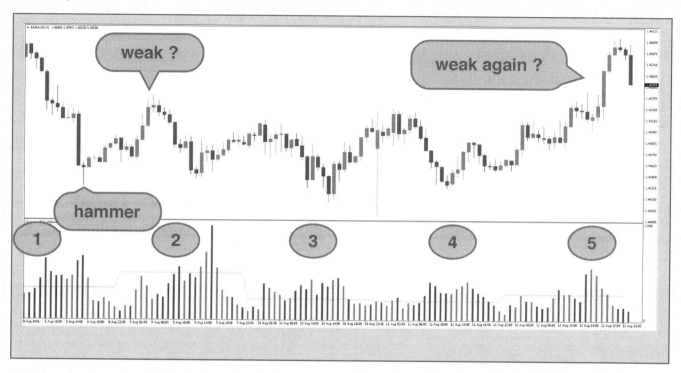

This is another chart where the comparative nature of the sessions helps to provide context for the volume profiles as we move from one phase of price action to another.

In this example the volumes across the sessions are much the same with only an increase in session two.

If we start to the left of the chart and session one, we have a nicely developed price waterfall which finally comes to an end on the hammer candle with the market makers stepping in to buy.

This is classic stopping volume, and in this case is unusual, as the rally begins almost immediately as it generally takes both time and effort for the market makers to absorb this degree of selling pressure, but here it is absorbed in the hour.

The rally into session two looks a little weak with the three up candles all topped off with wicks, and on volume that is falling with the final candle at the top simply adding further weight to the analysis.

This weakness is then confirmed with a second waterfall on rising volume, and a classic piece of volume price analysis action with the price spreads widening on rising volume.

The remaining sessions are then punctuated with further buying and selling within the consolidation phase with volumes generally declining slowly.

Finally in the last session we see the rally develop, but again note the volume. Once again we have a classic anomaly with the pair rising rapidly, but on falling volume, and one that is unlikely to move far.

EUR/CAD - 60 minute chart

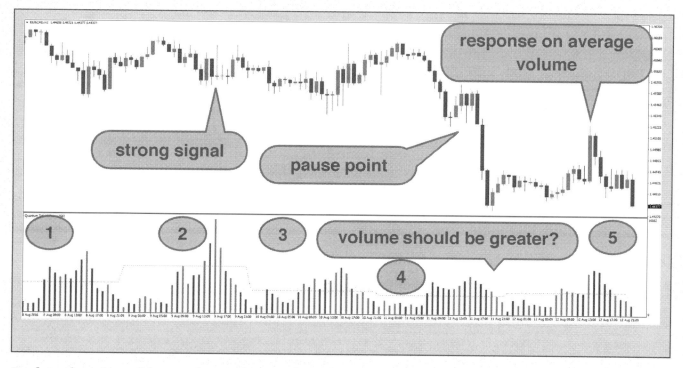

Back to the 'p' word here, where p is for patience. This is hard to follow at times, but when a market or currency pair is developing a well defined area of congestion, patience is generally rewarded, and as I have said many times before, time is the key here because the longer a market is in congestion, then the stronger the trend is likely to be once it starts.

This is enshrined in Wyckoff's second law of cause and effect, and the analogy I always use here is of a clockwork toy car. Winding the spring takes time, and the longer it takes the more energy is stored in the spring. When the toy is released, all the energy is released.

If the spring is fully wound then it will travel a great deal further, but if only partially wound, it will travel less far. This is the concept of time in the law of cause and effect. The greater the cause (in other words 'time') then the greater will be the net result (the effect).

The ceiling of resistance on this chart is extremely well defined, and session two confirms the campaign the market makers are building here with the ultra high volume bar and associated shooting star sending a strong signal of forthcoming weakness.

Further candles later in this session, and into session three, simply reinforces this view, before session four sees the price waterfall develop on rising volume and widening spreads. A text book example!

The pause point comes, but with no follow through and the waterfall gains momentum. However, note the volume here, it is now falling and so we have an anomaly of falling price and falling volume so we do not expect the pair to fall much further.

And in addition, note the spreads of the three down candles, which are all wide, and we should expect to see higher volume than is on the chart. Therefore, we can conclude this is not going much further.

The rally on session five is muted, and the contextual aspect of the volume profiles help to frame this in terms of a major reversal or simply profit taking.

The move lower resumes, and a break below the new floor of support is likely to see further downside momentum.

Congestion phases also introduce the elements of support and resistance, which are a key plank of all technical analysis and also of volume price analysis. These are the areas where trends are born. They are created during minor pauses in the secondary trend, and more major areas during the selling and buying climaxes which appear on all charts and in all timeframes.

And once one of the areas of resistance or support has been breached, volume then helps to confirm whether the breakout is genuine or false.

EUR/CHF - 60 minute chart

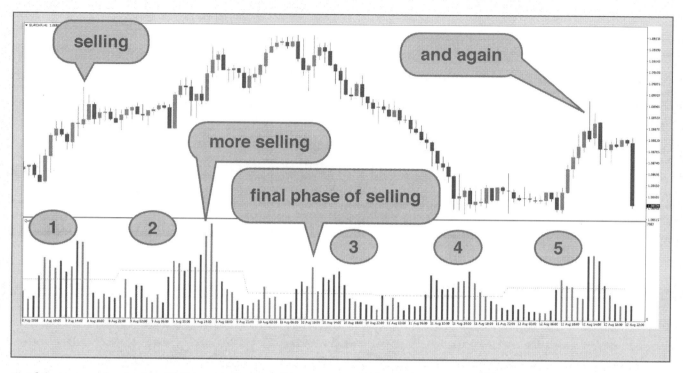

In this example timing is key, and several great examples of volume price analysis in action.

The first session sees the pair rise, but note the weakness which appears on high volume, a sign of some serious weakness! However, the market makers are not quite ready just yet.

Session two sees some further bullish momentum, but note the peak of the volume profile with the market makers selling into weakness once again on ultra high volume.

This is the highest volume of the chart and note the spread of the candle, it is compressed with a deep wick to the upper body and merely adds further weight to our analysis the market makers are preparing for a campaign lower, and selling here in preparation for such a move.

The upwards trend continues into session three, but is now looking increasingly weak, as the final phase of selling by the market makers on high volume takes place on the high of the session with the deep wick candle and narrow body.

The stage is set and the campaign begins with the price waterfall developing into session four.

Finally in the last session of the week, we see the pair rally, but note the associated volume.

We have a rising market and falling volume so this is not going too far, and at the top of the rally this is confirmed with a very strong signal as the volume soars and the candle closes as a shooting star with a deep wick to the upper body.

The outcome here is inevitable, and the pair reverses and the bearish primary trend is re-established once more, and down we go again.

EUR/GBP - 60 minute chart

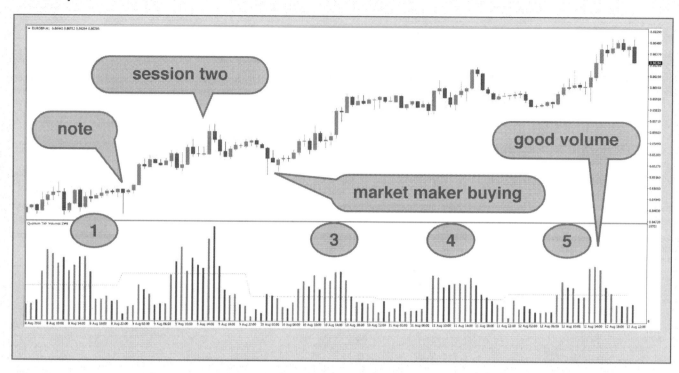

The interesting phase of price action for the EUR/GBP chart occurs in session two.

Session one sees the pair in congestion with some typical saw tooth price action and associated volume, but note the candle with the deep wick on very low volume.

A test into an area of previously high volume. Whilst this was between sessions and probably in a period of thin liquidity, nevertheless, significant due to the preceding area of high volume.

The pair then break higher in session two, but the rally looks weak and is interspersed with high volume on candles with wicks to the top of the body.

Weakness then appears on the high of this session with the narrow spread up candle and ultra high volume with the pair selling off. However, note the associated volume in the move lower, it's falling and suggesting a lack of downside momentum.

This is the classic anomaly of falling price and falling volume.

The rally higher is on low volume, but then session three begins with further buying by the market makers confirming their intent to move the pair higher still.

Note the deep wick to the lower body of the candle on average volume, and repeated two candles later with the pair then rising on generally rising volume, and supporting the rally higher.

Session four sees the pair move into a congestion phase, before session five sees the pair break higher on good volume, and on up to the next level as bullish sentiment continues to develop the primary trend.

EUR/NOK - 60 minute chart

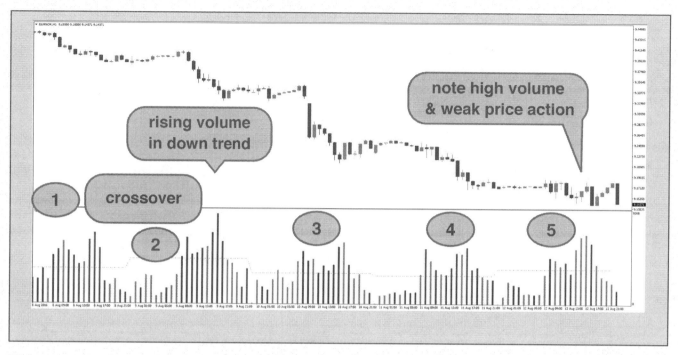

The euro Norwegian Krone cross is another pair where the price of oil is likely to play an influential role, and even a cursory glance at this chart reveals bearish sentiment purely based on the number of down candles and up candles on the chart.

The crossover between session one and session two is light in volume as expected, with session two then getting underway and reinforcing the bearish picture with rising volume in the down trend.

This is the classic relationship we are always looking for in a strongly bearish trend and sending a clear signal of a continuation 'longer term'.

The late rally on falling volume at the end of this phase of price action reinforces the weak picture, before session three picks up the trend once more, with rising volume in the falling market.

Note also the gap down in session three which further reinforces the bearish outlook.

Session four adds further to the bearish picture before session five finally brings a pause point to the extended move lower.

However, note the high volume in session five on the three initial up candles with the market makers slapping the market lower, before a repeat performance late in the session, and given the weak picture and heavy selling in session five, expect more to come in the longer term.

<u>My Notes</u>

EUR/SEK - 60 minute chart

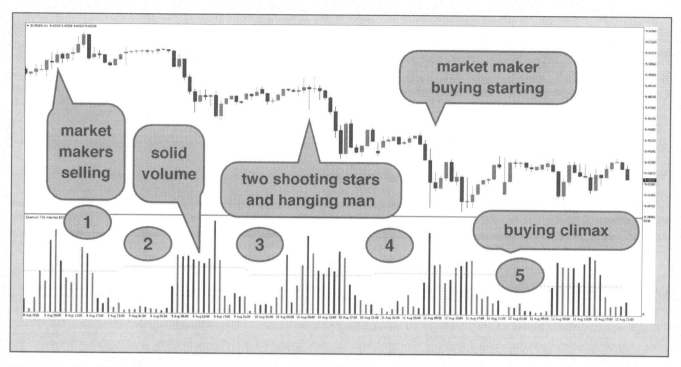

The euro Swedish Krona is not a heavily traded pair, but once again is a pair where volume price analysis can be perfectly applied in all timeframes.

If we start in the first session once again, here we see weakness building in the move higher, with the highest volume of this session then appearing on a narrow spread up candle. The market makers are struggling here and selling heavily into a weak market. At the top of this rally we see further selling on high volume and a narrow spread candle once again.

The bearish engulfing candle then follows, and sends a further confirming signal this pair is looking weak.

The overnight session is very quiet as the pair move into a very tight range, before volume picks up in session two, and the bearish trend gathers momentum and pace.

Session three then sees further weakness develop, and here we can see two shooting star candles on high volume with a hanging man candle sandwiched between.

The hanging man candle on high volume is sending a strong signal that selling is once again hitting the market, but the market makers are not ready just yet, and sell again.

We then see a repeat of the hanging man, this time smaller than the first and adding further confirmation to the weakness now building which duly develops on the next candle, and on into the price waterfall on rising volume.

Following a quiet period in the Far East and Asia, we see buying starting to appear from the market makers in session four with the wide spread down candle with a deep wick to the lower body and very high volume.

Here the market makers are now stepping in to buy to stop the pair falling further as session five sees the congestion build. The price action here is developing into a potential buying climax.

Note how each down candle fails to make any progress lower before the pair rally on good volume, suggesting the market makers are now preparing to reverse the primary trend from bearish to bullish.

GBP/AUD - 60 minute chart

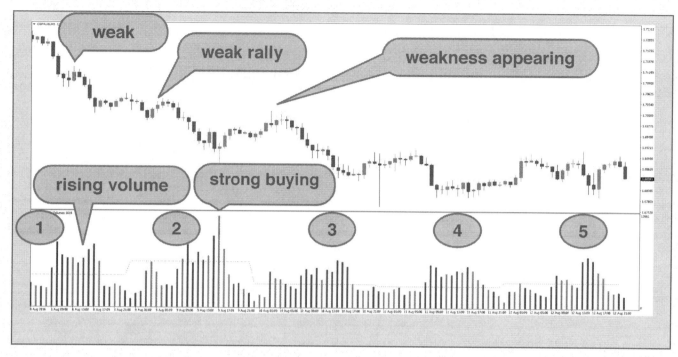

Another chart with some classic price action for the GBP/AUD.

And if we begin at the very left of the chart in the first session, here we have a classic example of the price waterfall, with the market falling on rising volume and good spreads, and the point to note here is the attempt to rally before the second phase of selling begins.

Here we see the narrow spread up candle on high volume, and a classic signal of further weakness to come. In any price waterfall, these are the candle and volume combinations to look for as an entry point if the initial entry was missed.

They confirm this market is weak, and the market makers are simply selling into weakness here, as buyers step in believing the down move is over, before the institutions take the market lower in their campaign.

Session two begins with a weak rally on falling volume - this is not going far, and a classic example of the secondary trend within the primary trend. In other words, the primary trend is likely to be re-established shortly.

As expected, the trend lower restarts with rising volume before strong market maker buying arrives on the highest volume of the session on a deep hammer candle. The rally follows on the crossover and into session three, before we see a weak shooting star candle on average volume, and now patience is required.

The waterfall then continues on rising volume before the final two sessions move the pair into an extended phase of congestion on average volume.

However, with the tone now set, and no strong signals of market maker buying, the bearish sentiment remains firmly in place and provided the support platform is broken, further downside price action should follow.

GBP/CAD - 60 minute chart

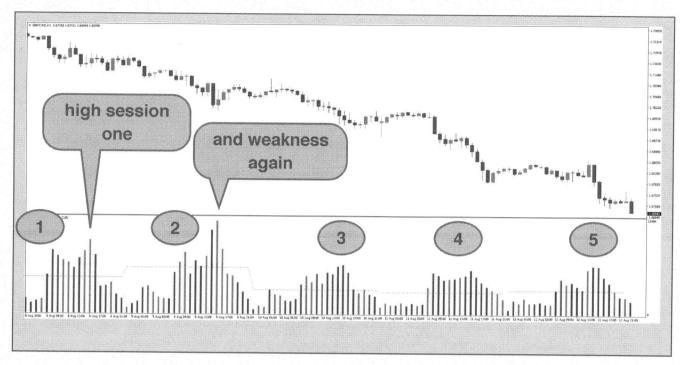

A very similar chart to the previous one, which is typically what we would expect in a commodity cross pair, but the GBP/CAD is also influenced by oil by virtue of the Canadian dollar.

Not so dramatic perhaps, but some of the key candles here are in the earlier sessions where volume is heavier.

Note the high of session one, with the narrow spread up candle on high volume, which is clearly not a bullish sign.

And we can be assured the market makers are selling heavily here into an already weak market, so it is only a question of time before the bearish momentum takes hold.

The same occurs in session two where once again the market attempts to rally, on even higher volume this time, but the market makers sell into the weakness on the highest volume of the session, with the rally looking very weak on declining volume.

The classic rising price and falling volume of the secondary trend is so powerful and reveals so much. This gives confidence in holding any position to maximise profits from the developing trend.

The downwards trend picks up momentum in sessions four and five, and with no evidence of market maker support or serious buying, this is a low probability trade on the follow through into the next session.

This would also be reflected on the 4 hour and daily charts with the various levels of support and resistance coming into play on a multi timeframe approach.

GBP/CHF - 60 minute chart

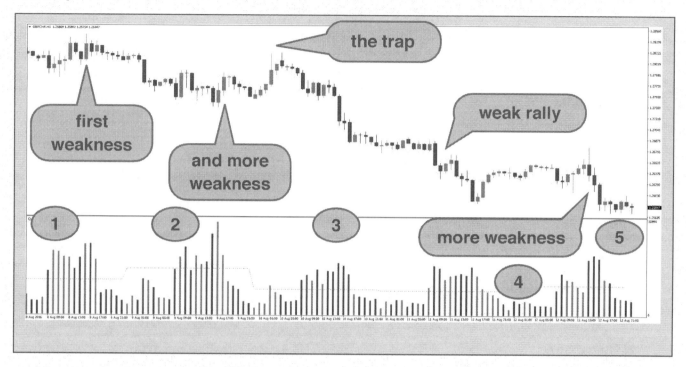

And here we have two further charts for the British pound and whilst the general trend is the same, the timing lags behind the two earlier examples.

As we can see the GBP/CHF pair managed to remain rangebound in the first two sessions, but the weakness is there, and it is only a question of time.

Weakness appears first in session one, with the up candle and wick to the top on the highest volume of the session. The market fails to follow through, or break above the resistance level.

Session two then delivers further weakness as the market makers sell into a another up candle on ultra high volume. The pair should have moved more than this - it hasn't.

Then session three begins with a wonderful trap move on low volume - the up candle with the deep wick to the upper body. This is a favourite trick of the market makers to trap traders into thinking the market is moving higher, and fast.

But it is doing neither, as they themselves are not participating. It is an illusion created to trap traders into weak position. This type of price action is often rapid, and designed to trigger the emotion of missing out.

The rally of session four looks very weak with increasing volume on the two up candles failing to deliver any upwards momentum, and so it proves in session five with the deep wick candle on high volume confirming further weakness to come as the market makers continue selling into weakness.

The market makers are not buying yet, so expect more of the same as this campaign has some way to run.

GBP/NZD - 60 minute

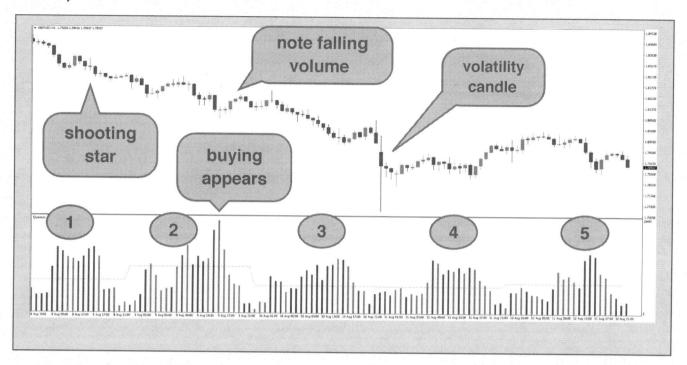

And the New Zealand dollar completes the set for the GBP commodity dollar cross pairs.

Again a similar picture here, and the weakness is confirmed in session one, with high volume associated with a shooting star candle as the market attempts to rally. Further weakness is confirmed in session two, but it is interesting to note the market maker buying which then appears mid way through the session and the market rallies higher.

However, this rally is weak. Note the narrowing spreads on the candles as they rise, and on their own a simple sign of weakness in any price chart, but here they are also associated with falling volume, so the anticipation is that this move is not going too far. Once again it is a secondary trend reversal against the primary bearish trend.

The only other highlight of this chart is the volatile candle of session three. Note the volume, or lack of volume. The market makers are not participating here so patience is required, as well as 'a wait and see' approach.

The rally higher is very weak, as judged with previous session volume, and the selling duly reappears in session five with good spread down candles and rising volume.

Once again the final rally is very weak on falling volume and narrowing spreads.

And the key for the longer term trend for this pair on this timeframe is then support and resistance which comes into play.

As the session comes to an end the pair is once again revisiting the floor of support now building in this area, and which will become pivotal as the next session unfolds. Any move through here on supporting rising volume will further confirm the bearish sentiment for the pair.

GBP/USD - 60 minute

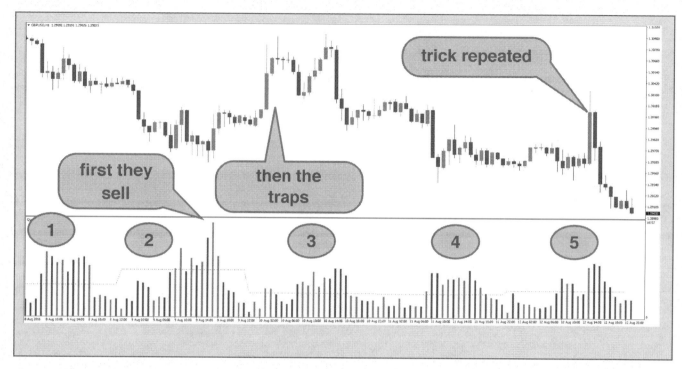

Finally we come to the majors and cable, and here we have some classic traps set for the unwary, or those traders who do not use volume in their analysis.

The traps are laid as we come out of session two and into session three.

First, the market makers need to sell and sell heavily which they do on the two up candles. The first on the high of the session, the second on reduced volume, and Cable then consolidates as volume falls at the end of the session. The ground has been prepared. Next come the traps.

First the volume in session three is generally below average, and we see a rapid move higher with a deep wick to the top of the candle.

The volume is very low and clearly this is a trap as we only have to compare this with that volume which has already been printed in sessions one and two.

The market makers continue with a second move higher.

Selling is absorbed and sold into the following five candles, all on average volume and with deep wicks to the upper bodies. And on average volume, the price is simply being 'marked up' by the market makers who are not participating.

Once set, the trap is sprung, and weak traders are left stranded at the highs. The trick is repeated in session five on the wide spread up candle.

After all following such a dramatic move in price, would we not expect to see some extreme volume here?

We have seen extreme volume earlier on the chart, and so should expect something similar here. But we do not, so it's no surprise to see the pair reverse immediately within two candles into a two bar reversal. And down we go with more bearish sentiment to follow.

NZD/CAD - 60 minute

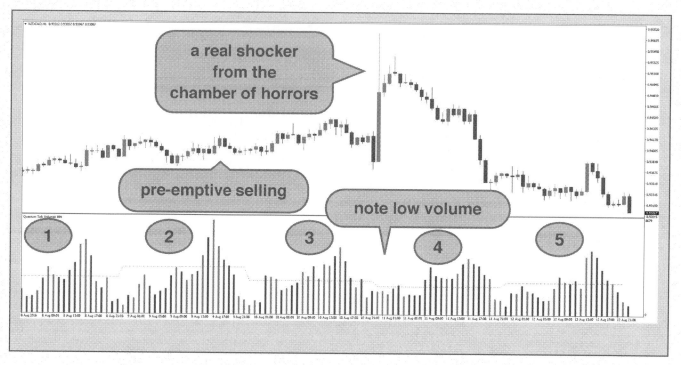

This is another chart straight from the chamber of trading horrors - a real shocker, so if you are of a nervous disposition, look away now.

There are anomalies, and then there are the anomalies we have here, and although I have referenced this on other charts, this is classic and worth repeating.

It offers us a great lesson, and perhaps is one of the strongest arguments I can put forward for learning how to interpret and apply volume price analysis. And this example should be sufficient evidence alone to convince anyone who is skeptical of its validity.

The focus, of course, is the major volatility candle in the centre of the chart, with virtually no volume to propel or justify such a move.

This is simply a classic trap move of epic proportions, and I wonder how many traders eagerly jumped onto this move, only to regret the decision, and then had to cover their positions as the market reversed.

And as always, the market makers prepare such campaigns with great care. Everything is planned in advance, and indeed much of the pre-emptive selling took place in session two, with the maximum volume associated with a weak candle.

Note also the candle immediately prior to the volatility candle, as the pair sells off strongly, but on low volume. Again this is a cynical ploy to draw traders into a short position too early, and then take them out on the rapid move higher.

Imagine how many would have placed stops on their short positions, only to see these triggered on the surge higher. Cynical, but an extremely profitable insider tactic.

It is interesting to note in sessions four and five how the subsequent selling volume falls away as the market has moved lower, so patience is required as the next move develops.

And as always support areas will now come into play.

NZD/JPY - 60 minute

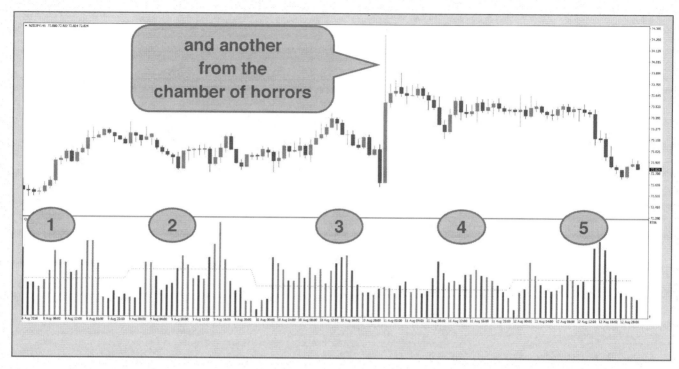

Much the same picture here so I won't labor the point, and indeed this chart offers us another lesson, and one that applies to many such moves in the forex world, and the point is this.

When trading one currency pair it always pays to watch related pairs. There are many reasons for this, not least because of the universality of flows in and out of a currency.

But there is also another reason, as the volume profiles associated with particular price action can also be very revealing, and can appear across the pairs, and here we have a case in point. A check on price action of the other Kiwi pairs would have confirmed this anomaly, and also confirmed (just as importantly) the extreme price reaction was not a glitch on the system.

Glitches do happen, and can be broker specific from time to time, so it is always worth checking to make sure this is not the case.

My Notes

USD/CAD - 60 minute

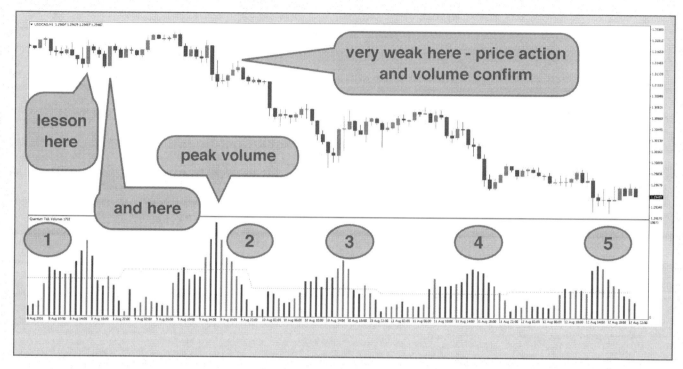

Some solid price action here for the USD/CAD, and if we start with session one, and an interesting lesson here on the two consecutive up candles that follow one another in relatively quick succession.

Both are the same size, and both follow within a short period, giving us an excellent comparative measure. The first is on high volume, and second is on average volume. So what is the lesson here?

And the lesson is the price action and volume suggests a lack of participation and lack of interest. After all, the price action is the same, in the same area, and yet on the second candle, the volume is light.

Clearly buying interest has waned here, and the market makers would have taken note. The tactic is to ease the market first higher on low volume through the Far East and Asia session, before off we go on rising volume as the market moves lower and into session two.

Note the peak of volume on the candle in session two with an attempt to rally, but the candle closes with a deep wick to the upper body.

Once again we see a rally rising on falling volume, which confirms this weakness, with session three then picking up the baton of sentiment. Note also the price action in the rally which always helps to confirm such weakness.

Here the spreads are narrow as the price action rises, and in addition the last two candles have wicks to the upper body, so are both strong signs of further weakness to come. And once weakness has been signaled by earlier candles, such a rally within the 'framework' of weakness can be a huge confidence boost as it is further confirmed with the volume.

Further selling then develops, as we move down into the congestion phase of session five with no sign of any buying by the market makers just yet.

USD/SEK - 60 minute

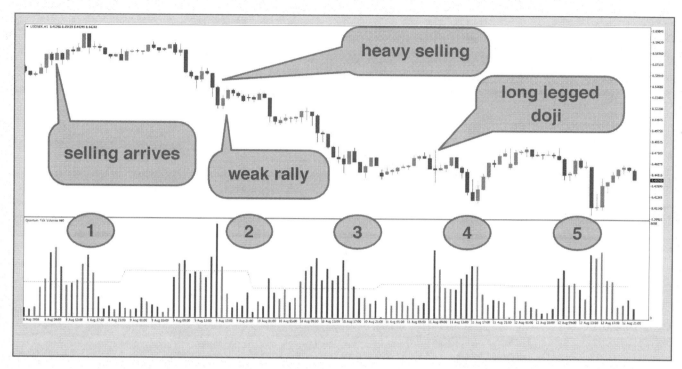

Another bearish chart where session one laid the groundwork, and the subsequent sessions simply followed the longer term trend.

In this example the initial selling by the market makers arrived early with the high volume of the session on the narrow spread up candle, and later confirmed with a clear two bar reversal on good volume.

The trend lower then begins with heavy selling pressure rising, before a weak rally on falling volume tries to bring the move to a halt.

This fails as selling pressure builds once again in session three, with the market makers moving in to buy before distributing again in the two bar reversal immediately after.

The long legged doji candle in session four is interesting, as it does signal insider participation, but with no clear direction, and whilst the initial move is to the downside, this is immediately reversed and takes the USD/SEK back into the congestion area.

This is repeated in session five, so further congestion awaits with patience now required as we wait for the next move to develop from this region.

Note however in the final session how the rally seems to lack conviction, with narrow spreads developing once again and on high to above average volume, so this looks weak.

In addition the price also ran into the resistance created by the congestion, so adding further weight to this analysis.

USD/TRY - 60 minute

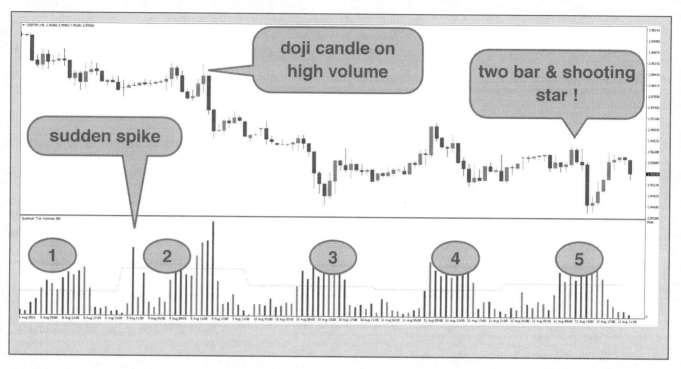

And onto one of the exotic currency pairs with the Turkish Lira.

Not perhaps quite as free flowing as the majors and cross currency pairs, but nevertheless volume price analysis provides the insight to trade these less liquid pairs with confidence.

Session two is perhaps the most interesting with the sudden spike in volume on an extremely small spread candle suggesting weakness ahead, that was duly delivered on the down candle on the highest volume of the period.

Note also the doji candle preceding the two wide spread down candles.

We have high volume and wicks to top and bottom. And whilst the direction cannot be guaranteed off this candle, the volume spike earlier in the session gives us a clue the break is likely to be to the downside and not to the upside.

We can also be assured the market makers are participating here, but have to wait for confirmation of direction.

There is never a guarantee of direction when trading, which is a reason why looking to the left of the chart all the time can help to provide confirming signals of what you are perhaps seeing at the live edge, and which may not be immediately clear. And a doji candle such as this is one example.

My Notes

USD/ZAR - 60 minute

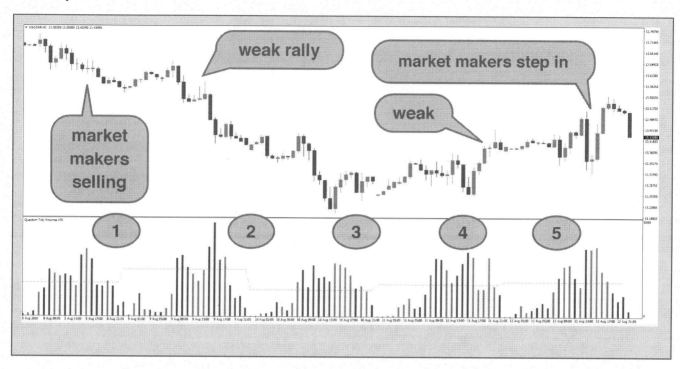

Finally in this section of pairs on the 60 minute timeframe we come to the USD and South African Rand pair which is popular, as it is one of the many currency pairs that offers higher yields, but one which can also be very volatile.

It is a pair which is also sought out when risk on sentiment is prevalent. So it can and does move very quickly, but is also likely to reverse just as fast.

Session one is weak, with the initial support from the market makers then converted into selling on session high volume with two repeated efforts to rise confirming one another.

Session two sees a weak rally, and is again one where the price alone gives strong hints as to the fragile nature of the market.

This is followed by heavy selling on rising volume, which continues into session three, but then subsides as the volume moves to average levels.

The subsequent rallies higher do look weak, but nevertheless are sustained with the market makers moving in during the mid point of session five.

They buy following the selling pressure in the down candle, and drive the market higher, but on falling volume once again.

The rallies look weak, and given the lack of market maker accumulation or significant buying, a further move lower seems likely, and of course much will also depend on the broader context of the USD, and its tone for this pair.

Section Three - 15 minute charts

In this section we move to the 15 minute timeframes and once again all these examples are from the MT4 platform.

Here the comparative nature of volume across sessions becomes less of an issue, other than when we are at the crossover itself. For example, when we move from the Far East and Asia into the London session, we do have to be careful in making any comparative judgements between the two.

There is a workaround here, which is to have enough of the chart displayed so we can compare the volume at the start of the London session with the start of the prior day's London session.

This gives us our benchmark, and so we are comparing volume in the same session. As the first few candles build we can then look back and compare volume in the same session.

In addition, another way to deal with this issue is we can step down to a faster timeframe, and use this as a quick reference guide to how volume is building on our fifteen minute chart as the session unfolds.

Worked Examples

AUD/CAD - 15 minute

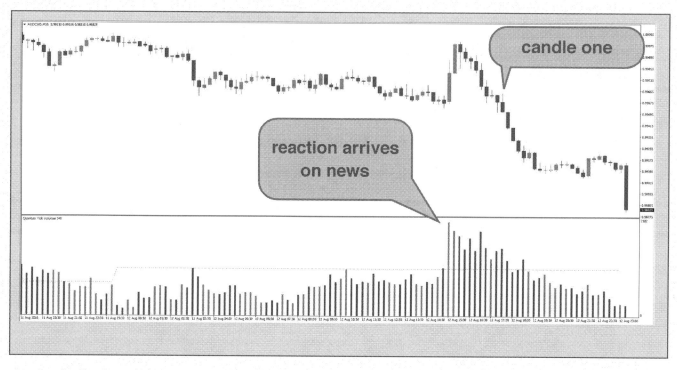

Having looked at a series of examples on the hourly chart, it's now time to drop down to a faster timeframe and look at volume price analysis in action on some 15 minute charts.

And as with all price action, this is simply an expanded view of the hourly chart, as well as a compressed view from the other end of the telescope, namely a fifteen minute chart.

For the first part of the chart, the AUD/CAD pair drifts lower with volume rising and falling gently through the various phases. Then the reaction arrives on high volume with two strong up candles which looks very positive, but the following candle reflects weakness as it is a hanging man.

In this case there is no precursor of weakness, so whilst it is easy to make this judgement with hindsight, leading edge analysis would have been more difficult, as at this point you could not be certain on direction.

However, once the waterfall develops it is on high volume and on breaking below the platform of support, then invites a lower risk trade with a more certain outcome.

The two candle reaction higher was almost certainly on news, and at such times it pays to wait and be patient and either trade the fade or wait for confirmation of the trend.

The trigger for joining the move here might have been the break below support, and in addition we also have some strong signals lower down in the price waterfall, such as at candle one.

This is the classic 'attempt to rally' with the market makers selling heavily into the weakness, thereby creating the wick to the upper body of the candle.

Then off we go again. So always keep an eye out for this type of candle, and when supported with good volume, can provide a confident entry point, or even the opportunity to scale in.

AUD/CHF - 15 minute

Here we have a similar price chart to the previous one, before an injection of volume over a three candle arrangement comes in, but for this pair, the weakness is much clearer.

The first candle is indecisive, and it is impossible to judge which way the market is going to react to the volatility (probably from news) given the violent oscillation, and deep wicks to both top and bottom, so patience is required.

Then we see the second candle. Again we have very high volume, but on a narrow doji candle which looks more promising.

Then the third candle arrives, again on very high volume, but the spread is narrow.

After such an injection of volume we should have expected to see the market jump higher, not least because we have seen the same price spread achieved with less than half this volume earlier in the session, therefore we can conclude the insiders are selling here, and also selling in the preceding two candles. And the hanging man also confirms this view.

The waterfall then develops, before we move into a short congestion phase, and it is at this point that any decision to enter could be taken. As we have seen in several other examples, the key candle is the weak attempt to rally on good volume.

This is where the market makers are selling into weakness. Remember too, there are many traders who always buy on dips, so there is always a plentiful supply of willing customers for the market makers.

This is always a nice signal to see, and will give you the confidence to join a move which is underway, and at a congestion phase. The volume under this candle is high, and it is therefore only a question of time before the move lower continues.

Here it is on the next candle. It may take longer, but these are great signals in the down trend, and great confidence builders.

AUD/JPY - 15 minute

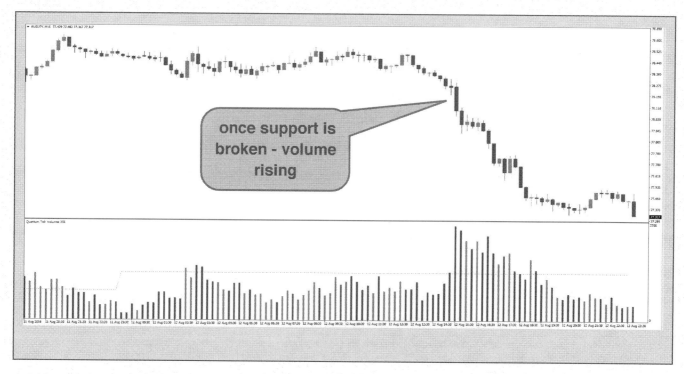

Patience, patience, patience...it always pays off in the end, but is so hard to do! Here is a great example where patience is rewarded, and the chart requires little in the way of an explanation.

But, I would say is this.

The key is to wait for the support or resistance level to be breached, and then consider the volume. In this case, once it has been broken, the volume starts to rise in classic fashion with wide price spreads developing and confirming the bearish trend, and once this is underway, it is simply a case of deciding where and when to take a position in the market.

The rallies look very weak, and there is no diminution of volume in the down trend. However just as important, there is no evidence of any market maker buying either.

Volume will always give you the confidence to enter these positions, and all that is required is patience, which is the most difficult part.

My Notes

AUD/USD - 15 minute

And so to the Aussie major, and whilst you may think the price action here is the same as before, there is one important difference.

Here we have a news release, and two 15 minute candles, with the volume on the second candle only marginally lower than on the first candle. Is this important? And the answer is most definitely yes.

The first candle has seen the price move by a factor of five, with this amount of volume. But the second candle has only moved by a factor of two with an almost identical amount of volume. So is this a good sign or a bad sign?

Clearly, something is not right here. If the first candle is the yardstick for our volume, then the second candle looks weak, and would suggest the market makers are selling heavily.

Indeed the wick of the first candle hints at weakness and selling, but is more likely profit taking by those who took positions ahead of the news.

The second candle has a smaller wick, but it is the volume which is the key point here and the spread of the candle which is so much smaller than the first.

The third candle then arrives, and is a hanging man on high volume. The first sign of selling which the market makers then move in to buy to 'prop up' the market.

Then the price waterfall develops with a typical weak rally on high volume at the first stopping point in the move lower, once again giving us a strong signal for any entry.

In addition this also gives the confidence to hold if the entry was taken higher in the move, as well as the option to scale in. Either way, the application of volume price analysis will either help you to stay in and maximise any profit, or enter with confidence and then build a position. Both are equally important.

CHF/JPY - 15 minute

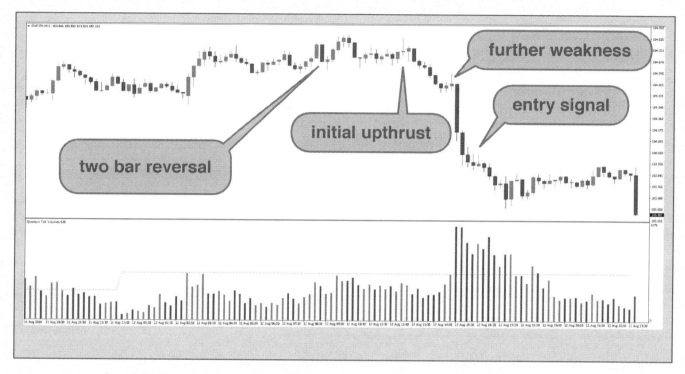

A neat example of the break out trade, and again one where patience is required.

Congestion breakout trading gets a bad press, but if the move is corroborated with volume, this confirms whether the breakout is true or false.

The preceding price action gives us various clues and signals along the way, but with the two bar reversal, wick topped candles, and generally weak volume on the rallies higher, the ceiling of resistance looks to be building.

And again we have a clear example of the upthrust in secondary congestion which signals weakness, and the subsequent move lower.

But please don't think for one moment these will always appear - they do not, and not as helpfully as here with the market breaking lower following the hanging man which comes immediately after.

Nevertheless, they are extremely strong and valuable signals and when confirmed with high volume, even more so.

And indeed as I was writing, I then noticed a further signal at the next pause point below on even higher volume. And the reason these appear is very simple.

It is the market makers selling into weakness, and preparing for the next leg down.

So keep an eye out for these signals in the price waterfall - they are invaluable and great confidence builders.

EUR/AUD - 15 minute

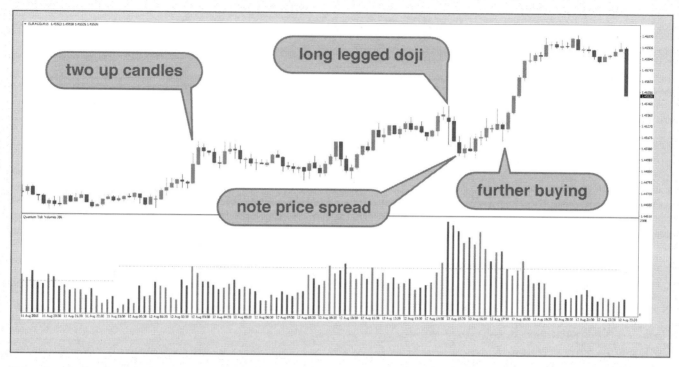

It's nice to be looking at some price action going the other way this time, but a tough chart to read. It is easy to read with hindsight, but not so easy at the live edge of the market, so let's take a look.

The first period of price action is more straightforward. The move away from congestion on the left looks a little weak on falling volume, but is supported with average volume on the pause, before moving higher with the up candles on average volume.

A further long congestion phase then follows, with a two bar reversal capping gains, before we see a further weak rally up and into the major volume area.

First comes a long legged doji candle on extreme volume, which is followed by two down candles on high volume. However, note the second candle and spread which is much narrower than the first.

If the first candle and volume is our benchmark here, then the second candle, on much the same volume, is suggesting buying here by the market makers.

After all, if they were selling, then the spread of the candle should be much the same as the first.

It is not - in fact it is half the size on similar volume and so gives us a strong signal the market makers have stepped in to buy. There is no wick to mention to the bottom of the candle, but this is not always the case as we can see here.

This view is further confirmed by the following candle, which is narrow in spread, but on very high volume.

This certainly confirms the market makers are buying once again, and the following candle adds further weight. This is a signal of buying and is much the same as a gravestone candle at the bottom of a significant fall.

It is the same here, with buying now appearing, and confirmed with further buying as we get underway in the trend higher.

EUR/CAD - 15 minute

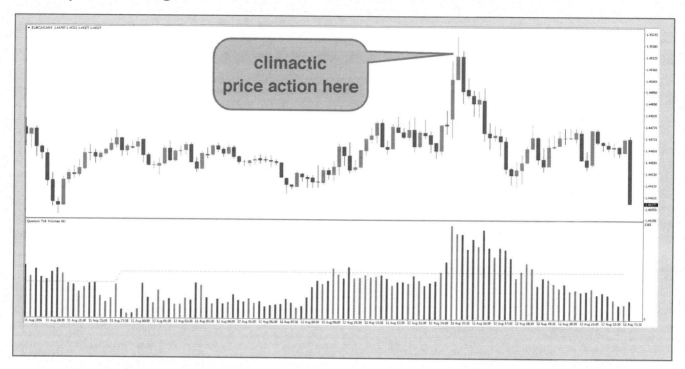

The focus of attention here is on the climactic volume towards the right of the chart.

Once again the price action reveals a great deal, but it is volume that gives us the complete picture.

The first candle forms on ultra high volume, but with a wick to the top and bottom, so we certainly have strong buying, but with some indecision and selling.

But one thing we can be sure of is the market makers are certainly participating in the price action. The next candle then builds, and closes with a deep wick to the top, with the close coming half way down the candle.

On such high volume this is a strong signal of weakness. As always try to imagine what this price action and volume profile would look like on a faster chart.

For example on fifteen one minute candles or three five minute candles, which would reinforce and expand the view of this single candle.

This candle is then engulfed, and the downside momentum begins on high volume, and is confirmed in the two wide spread down candles before we see the market makers step in at a lower level where some buying arrives, and we move into the classic congestion phase as the volume dies away.

And any strong move through the floor of support will then extend the bearish momentum further.

EUR/CHF - 15 minute

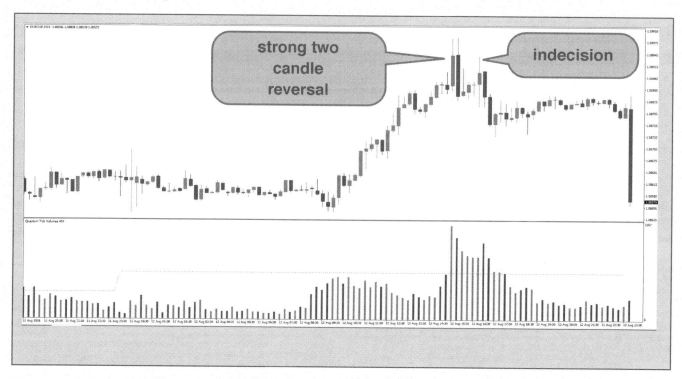

This example is similar to the previous one, but is one where the candle arrangement is slightly different. The result is much the same, although the bearish momentum fails to follow through to quite the same extent.

Remember also here, the surge in volume will have scaled back the preceding volume bars accordingly, so whilst it is below average on the chart, at the live edge, and ahead of the market market selling, it would have been above average and even high.

This is always important to remember when viewing charts in this way as extreme volume, as here, will always impact what has gone before, and of course, what comes after, and is a case of where we have to 'recalibrate' our view of volume as the future bars unfold.

This issue is also very common at the crossover periods, from the Far East and Asia into Europe and London, where we have to wait a few bars, before we can judge what is high, medium or low once more.

So in this case, the trend higher was a solid move, with only minor weakness towards the end as the volume trend gently declined in the move higher.

Remember too, the remit of the market makers is to make money for themselves and not you, and in doing so they know where they are heading next - in advance. You will often see this positioning ahead of any economic data or release.

If the market is moving strongly in one direction prior to the data release, it is often the case it will reverse on the news. And we would do the same given the chance.

On this chart we see another very strong two bar reversal with wicks to the top on high volume, but no follow through. Indecision follows, and then down we go, and into the congestion phase.

EUR/GBP - 15 minute

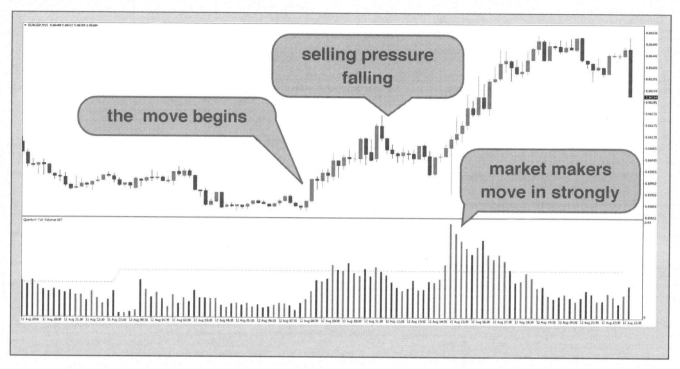

One of the facets we often forget as volume traders is the information conveyed in the congestion phase, and here we have some classic examples.

Yes, these are flattened a little by the surge later, but nevertheless are perfect examples of what I mean.

Whilst it is often obvious when we are in a congestion phase, the start of one may be less obvious, so what volume will confirm is the lack of participation by the market makers.

The section of price action to the centre of the chart describes this very well.

The narrow spreads are confirmed with very low volume. The two complement one another perfectly, and all that is required is patience. The price action reveals congestion, but the low volume reinforces the message for us.

The pair then breaks higher with selling pressure falling in the reversal, but note the volume.

Here we see a falling market and falling volume, before we see a huge injection of buying from the market makers as they move in strongly.

The market maker buying is self evident here on the highest volume of the session, on the very deep wick to the lower body of the candle.

Drag the market lower first, then buy and drive it higher fast - all on one candle. The drive higher is not straightforward as they are hit with selling on the way up, but they continue to drive the market higher and into the top on exhaustion volume.

EUR/JPY - 15 minute

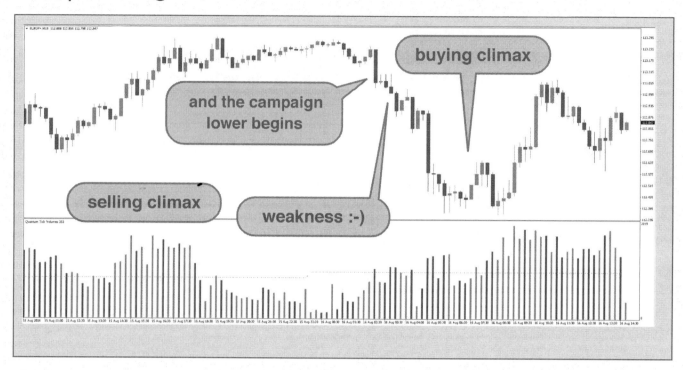

This is a great example where we can see all the climactic price action, and how it develops, and how it follows into the next phase of price action.

First we see the effort required to reach the top of the hill, the selling climax, and the exhaustion that follows as the market rolls over, and falls all the way back down again. It's what I refer to as the soufflé effect. The market rises quickly, and then collapses just as fast.

If we start at the left of the chart, the weakness in the rally becomes increasingly apparent the higher we go.

Note the steps as the pair move higher, with the down candles following each rally higher, but duly supported by the market makers, before they push the pair up to the next level. Effort to rise, and then the fall as sellers take their profit with the market makers stepping in to buy in order to take the move on up to the next level.

You can see this clearly depicted here. As the rally stalls, so the depth to the wick on the final candle signals buying from the market makers. The campaign has not been completed yet, and is reflected in the volume as they step in.

Then we move into the congestion phase, and the volume falls away. This is classic, and is often something we forget as volume traders.

Yes, we are always looking for the traps, the high and low volume, but when the congestion phase starts, look for confirmation in the volume. If the congestion is genuine then the market makers will be sitting it out, and waiting to start the next phase of the campaign.

Then we are off on rising volume as the primary bullish trend is reversed into a primary bearish trend. Note also in the trend lower how the small 'upthrust' candles confirm both the weakness now in place, and also provide excellent opportunities to join the trend as it develops. And down we go again with a repeat on the next rally.

The primary bearish trend then starts to come to an end as the market makers step in once more, this time to buy as stopping volume appears and we move into the buying climax at the bottom of the chart. This is the classic price action and associated volume we expect to see in the buying climax.

The deep wicks to the lower body of the candle signal market maker buying as momentum is removed from the move lower. Further mopping up then follows before we are off again into the next phase of price action, as the trend reverses once again.

This is the cycle of price action we see described in all timeframes, and is the classic Wyckoff cycle, from the selling climax, to the buying climax and back again, and described here in a very simple example on the 15 minute timeframe. But this could be any timeframe you care to choose.

EUR/USD - 15 minute

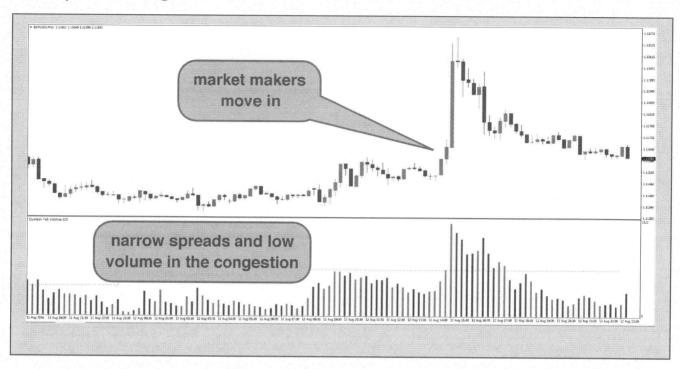

A further example of the relationship we expect to see between congestion and price action, not simply from a volume perspective but also from a price perspective which is just as important.

Throughout the congestion phase, the spreads remain narrow and on any reaction lower or higher the volume is in agreement here.

This simply confirms the market makers are not participating, but then neither are they playing any tricks, and whilst we tend to focus on the directional aspects of trading, trading a range is equally valid. It all depends on your strategy and tactics and what suits you.

in this example, we could be in a binary option, with a tunnel or a one touch, no touch. We could have an option in play, and waiting for an expiry.

We could have taken a position on the anticipation of volatility. All are valid.

Once this phase of price action comes to an end, it is signaled with insider participation as the institutional market makers move in strongly to drive the pair higher on very strong and rising volume, before topping out in classic style and reversing the pair almost immediately leaving many traders trapped at the top on the expectation of further upside momentum.

It's a cruel trick, which is why you need volume price analysis to help and guide you from the inside out, and this is such a clear illustration of the extremes of volume.

From the very low, and a lack of participation, to very high where the market makers are in full control.

The shooting star candle on extreme volume is a clear and unequivocal sign of weakness, which appears over the following phase of price action.

GBP/AUD - 15 minute

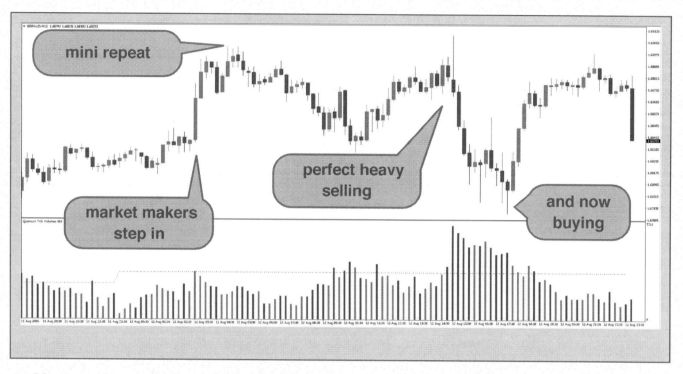

And here on the 15 minute chart for the GBP/AUD we have some further excellent lessons.

If we start at the left of the chart, the initial congestion phase builds before the market makers step in on the wide spread up candles, and inject some momentum into the move higher. However, three signs of weakness appear relatively quickly.

First the spreads are narrowing. Second the candles have wicks to the upper body, and third the volume is falling.

We then see a 'mini repeat' of this price action with the three up candles again on narrowing spreads, and on average volume that is relatively flat. In addition, the second candle in this sequence has a deep wick, with the third candle narrowing with wicks to both top and bottom.

The pair then weaken, and note the efforts to rise on very low volume in each minor rally as the move lower develops.

Finally, we see some buying appear with the rally, before the major selling commences with the very well defined shooting star candle on the highest volume of the session.

This signal is so clear it would be hard to miss, even for those traders with only a passing understanding of volume price analysis.

The waterfall starts with stopping volume then appearing as we reach the bottom, and the 'mopping up' phase commences, before we are off again to the upside.

But note the volume under the wide spread up candles - it is falling, and is only average, so this move looks to be running out of steam, which proves to the case.

GBP/CAD - 15 minute

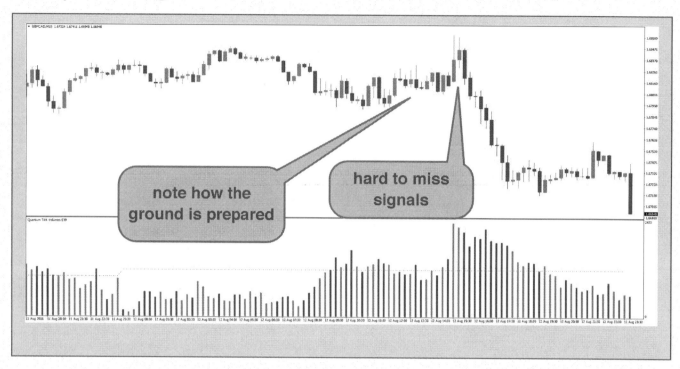

Another top which marks the end of an extended congestion phase, and the signals here are clear and unequivocal, and truly reveal the power of volume price analysis.

But what is also interesting here is the price action in the run up to the climactic volume as the market makers step in.

If you notice in the congestion phase, the price action already looks weak with wicks to the upper body of several candle as we approach the dramatic price action, which would have been associated with a news release or statement.

And it is naive to think the insiders and market makers do not have prior information of any news or data driven events, and you will often see this put to good effect prior to any release. The campaign here is to short the market, and the selling prior to the release is simply the market makers preparing the ground.

Then as the news is released they move the pair rapidly higher before selling into the weakness, and repeat this on the second candle, again on extreme volume. Such signals are so clear, and hard to miss, and confirmed immediately with the next candle, which is a wide spread down candle on high volume.

Once confirmed it is simply a question of when to enter a short position. After the initial down candle on high volume, which confirms the insider selling, should we enter before it starts, or after the price has broken through the support platform?

And here it is a personal decision based on individual risk appetite.

And with no stopping volume appearing at lower levels, it is also valid to wait and enter the trend as it develops further. There is no right or wrong answer, just the one that suits you, and your attitude to risk.

GBP/CHF - 15 minute

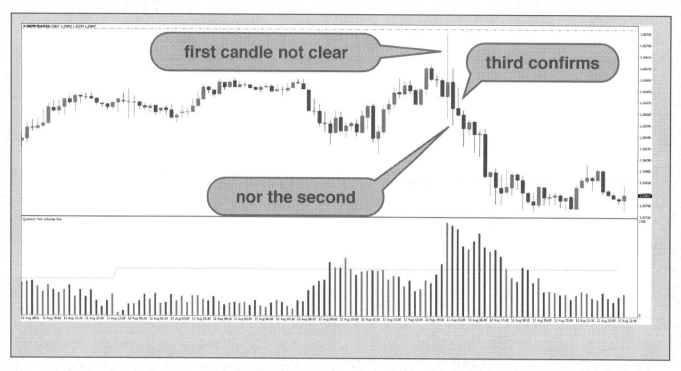

A similar example to the previous one, but not so clean and clear, and indeed this raises a further important point and it is this.

Often within a currency complex one chart for a pair may be less clear, whilst another may offer much clearer signals, or clarify what we see on our first chart.

Naturally this is not always the case, and also assumes the sentiment for the currency under consideration is universal across the complex.

But again this is not always the case. Nevertheless, this is always something to consider, and is another reason to use both multiple charts, and multiple pairs for validation and cross checking.

In this case, the first candle is perhaps not clear. We have extreme volume once more, but the candle has wicks to both top and bottom giving us a signal of indecision and from which any conclusions are hard to draw.

So we wait.

The next candle suggests bearish sentiment may be in the ascendancy given the extreme volume once more, but perhaps the wicks to top and bottom are of concern here.

The probability is it is heavy selling, so we have to be patient and wait. Candle three then really delivers the answer with no debate, and off we go on another strong move lower.

And as always after a strong move, the market then moves into a congestion phase.

GBP/JPY - 15 minute

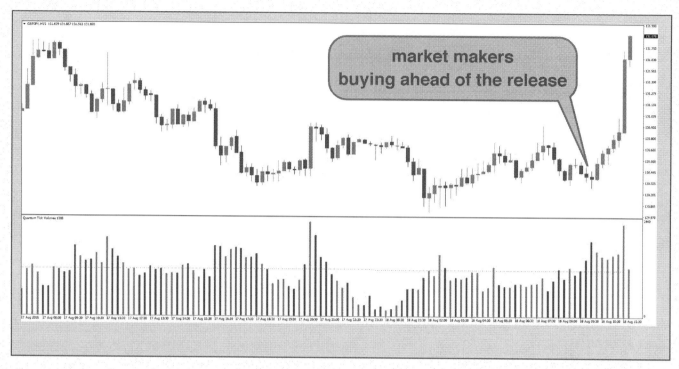

I've added this example as it was one I was trading at the time, and is also a perfect example of two things.

First, the market maker positioning ahead of news, and second the fact they have an insight into the release ahead of everyone else.

This should not be a surprise, and you will see this all the time.

The institutional market makers are like Japanese knotweed - their tendrils are everywhere, and it is difficult to imagine they would not have access to the details somewhere!

The focus here is on the right hand side of the chart, and the price action immediately preceding the rally. The news release was on the wide spread up candle.

However, note the three down candles, and the strongly rising volume. This is insider buying, and positioning ahead of the news.

What does this tell you? They are buying.

That's what it told me. So I bought too.

Then the rally started with the injection of momentum on the release itself, which was Retail Sales and Jobs on this occasion.

Surprisingly both were better then expected, and the pair soared higher on GBP buying.

You will see this all the time ahead of a release. So do the insiders and market makers have an insight on the data? What do you think.

GBP/NZD - 15 minute

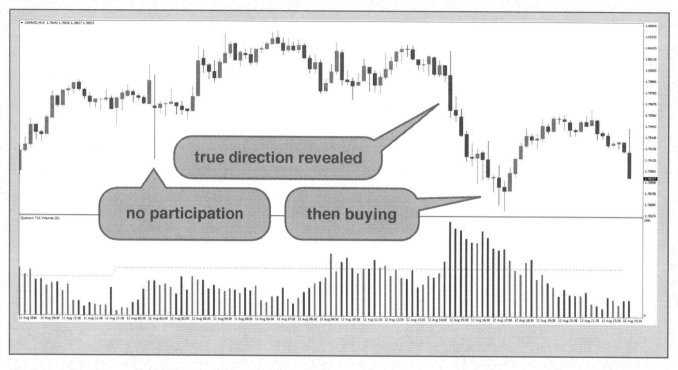

Doji candles come in all shapes and sizes, and the long legged form is just one type.

As I have said before, it is impossible to gauge market direction from this candle, which generally appears as a result of volatility on news, or from market maker manipulation or both.

The only conclusion we can draw is from the volume, but not make any assumptions on direction.

If the market makers are participating, then all we can conclude is simply that, and we must wait for them to reveal their hand with any move away from the price region.

If they are not involved, then the prospect is it is a trap, and armed with this knowledge we can then view the next phase of price action with a healthy degree of skepticism.

On this occasion, it was more a question of the latter rather than the former, with the GBP/NZD pair rising on falling volume, and the move containing several two bar reversals.

The true direction is only revealed as the market makers move in to sell heavily, before buying at the bottom to reverse the trend into congestion, and a short term rally higher.

But the rally higher is associated with falling volume, so it is no surprise to see this run out of steam as we approach the right hand side of the chart.

My Notes

GBP/USD - 15 minute

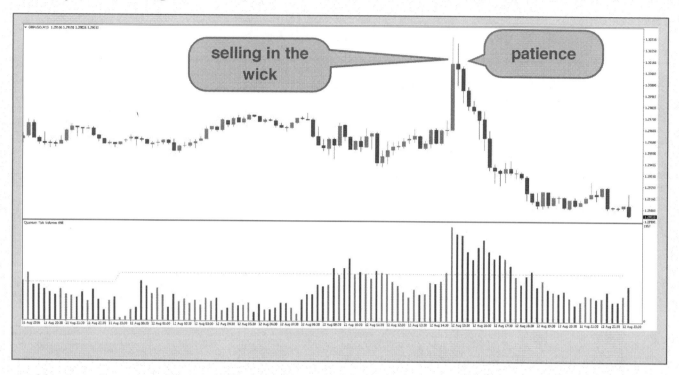

And here we have another example of the doji candle in action, and one where a little patience is required.

The congestion phase has built before the surge in volume arrives on the wide spread up candle which closes with a deep wick to the top. The market makers are in town.

This is a good solid candle with the highest volume of the day, but there is selling at the top with the wick.

This could simply be profit taking, so caution is required.

Then comes our doji candle. Is this buying or selling?

We cannot be sure so best to keep our powder dry for the time being. Then candle three arrives, and really confirms with strength that this is indeed selling, and the price waterfall then develops nicely.

Doji candles appear in all timeframes, and come in all shapes and sizes, and the larger they are the more difficult they are to read.

So don't try to do so. Wait for the trades to come to you. They will, and it's that word patience again.

And just to remind you once again, a doji candle is not a signal of a reversal. In this case it was, but this may or may not be the case when a candle such as this is created.

All it confirms is indecision, and we have to wait for the direction to be confirmed in due course.

NZD/CAD - 15 minute

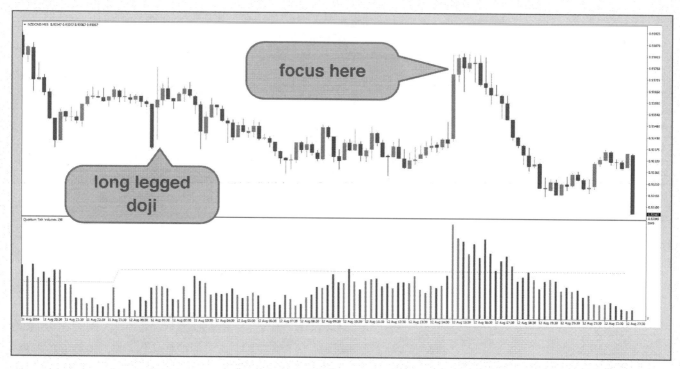

More long legged doji candles here also, but the price action I wanted to focus on is to the right of the chart as the market makers move in with volume.

And it is a chart where once again patience is required. In this case there is no reversal, and no particular change in trend, simply a continuation of the congestion phase, which has a mildly bearish tone building thereafter.

But when we move to the right of the chart and the first major up candle, this looks solid enough. We also have the highest volume of the session, and the wick to the top of the candle suggests profit taking which is to be expected after such a strong move.

The second candle then builds with no wicks this time, but the price action is substantially narrower than the previous candle.

And whilst this looks weak, we still cannot be sure. What we can be sure of is that this is an anomaly, because such effort should have seen the pair close with a much taller candle.

We have not, and so we can conclude this looks very weak.

The next candle then forms with the deep wick, but is this buying or selling here? Well the candle suggests a hanging man, and the first sign of selling. What is happening here is selling has arrived, but the insiders have bought the weakness in order to push the price back higher.

Then comes the narrow spread up candle with a wick to the top which is a more conventional sign of weakness given the substantial volume below.

Then comes another hanging man - increasing our belief this pair is preparing for a move lower. Then the first down candle appears on high volume, with a further much stronger signal confirming the previous candles, and closing with the deep wick candle alongside.

We are now primed, and ready for the move lower.

NZD/CHF - 15 minute

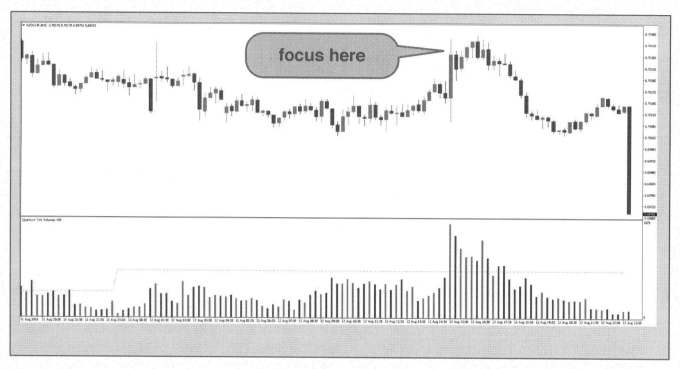

And I thought I would add this chart as a further example where we have to wait for some clearer signals to develop.

The initial extreme volume drives the market higher, but we have wicks to top and bottom, so the message here is not clear.

The following down candle hints at selling, but even here we have a wick to the lower body of the candle, not large, but enough to make us suspicious.

The market moves higher, but on relatively narrow spreads, before more selling appears, and at this point we would still not be certain.

Then the next up candle arrives with a narrow body and a wick to the top on much higher volume, and really does deliver a much stronger confirmation of weakness. But perhaps not enough.

This is followed by another down candle on good volume, a narrow spread candle on below average volume, a hanging man, and finally an upthrust on above average volume.

The market finally breaks, and at this point really does confirm the bearish picture. But this has taken almost three hours to build, and not something we might wish to wait for as a scalping trader.

As always, if you are not sure, wait for a more demonstrable candle with volume to appear. If it confirms - that's great. But if not, you have lost nothing.

NZD/JPY - 15 minute

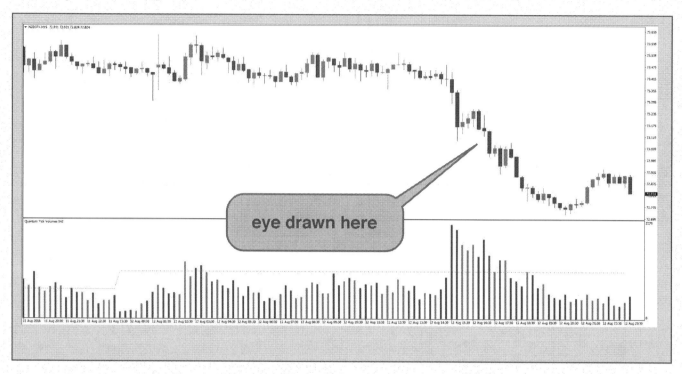

Once again it is the congestion phase where the trend is developed and launched, and once these areas begin to build, it is only a question of when, and not if, the market will then trend.

The NZD/JPY is also one of the primary pairs for the carry trade, and like other yen pairs will be subject to hot money flows as speculators seek out higher returns. And despite the 'race to the bottom' the NZD still retains some differential, but increasingly the exotics are being sought out to provide more attractive returns.

The candle my eye is instantly drawn to here is in the secondary congestion phase as the price waterfall begins.

After the initial two candle move lower, the pair rallies over three up candles. We then have a down candle, and finally the upthrust candle on very high volume, which is hugely significant given the preceding candle.

It is the final signal of the market makers selling into weakness before dropping the market once more. Hunt these candles out, and if the volume is high, they will give you the confidence to get in when you are ready, even if you missed the initial entry, or had decided to wait for the trend to develop.

My Notes

NZD/USD - 15 minute

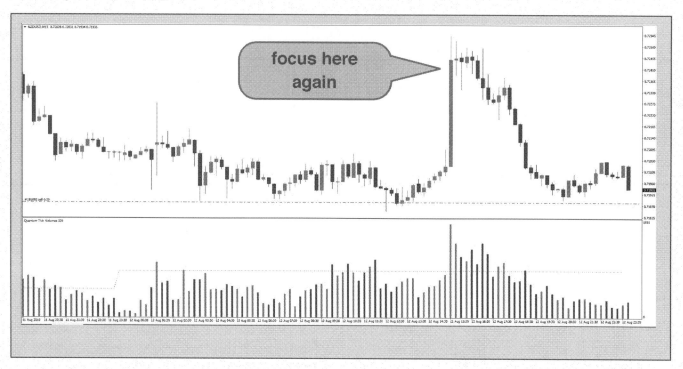

And further examples here in slightly different areas of the price waterfall.

The initial wide spread up candle is extreme, but the volume is ultra high so this looks fine, despite the wick to the top of the candle. However, the problem with all such extreme candles is deciding on the volume, and whether this is in agreement.

In other words, we have no immediate benchmark and given the preceding volumes, this looks a little 'lightweight'?

And remember this is another favourite trick - to move price outside of its average true range, and then reverse it almost immediately.

This candle is followed by a long legged doji candle but we cannot draw any conclusion, other than the market makers are participating.

There then follows a hanging man, highlighting weakness followed by a weak up candle, and a second hanging man. Now we have a strong sign of weakness. The first down candle appears followed by a big upthrust candle on high volume.

This really confirms the weakness, and on the recovery rally in the secondary phase, another upthrust candle appears on high volume.

145

The market falls fast, and ultimately into the congestion phase as the volumes subside.

Remember too with such wide spread candles, that when this type of action develops, with moves outside the average true range, price action will often revert inside the spread of the candle.

And the reason is because it is often associated with market maker participation, or a lack of participation, and will result in a subsequent reversal.

USD/CHF - 15 minute

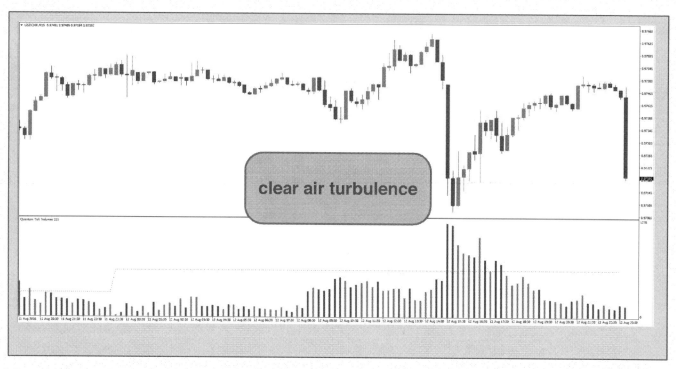

clear air turbulence

There is no warning here, either at the top or the bottom, so is a move that can best be described as clear air turbulence.

This could have been news or data so was probably expected, but nevertheless the reaction is instant, with the move ending in two major candles. There is no reaction higher and no pause or distribution areas, just an immediate drop in two candles.

Equally at the bottom there is little to suggest we are about to witness a strong recovery back to the original open of the move in a relatively short space of time.

And perhaps one of the most difficult things to do here is to trade in the rally higher. Because your emotional conscious mind will be reminding you of the speed of the fall.

And I included this example for just this reason.

Volume price analysis is not the panacea for every situation, and moves such as this can and do occur.

This was a tough one, and would have caught many traders out on both sides of the market.

The only way to trade such moves is by using multiple timeframes, which can help to provide an alternative perspective not only on the price action, but also the volume profiles, which will then offer that all important 'alternative view'.

I cannot stress this too strongly, as considering charts in more than one timeframe then gives us a very different perspective and will reveal so much more than a single chart.

USD/MXN - 15 minute

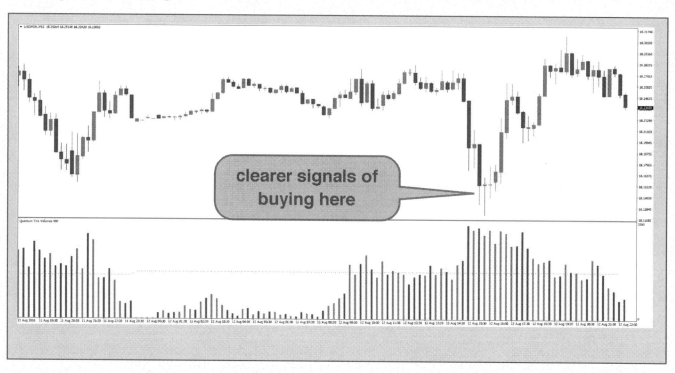

And here we have an exotic pair where so much more is likely to occur.

Once again it is the move lower which takes hold immediately. The long legged doji candle at the pause point is not helpful, other than to signal market maker participation.

And the move continues lower on another wide spread candle on ultra high volume.

Finally, on this occasion we do receive a much clearer signal as a deep hammer candle on very high volume signals the market makers moving in to buy heavily, and after a short pause on another doji candle, drive the market higher and quickly on very high volumes.

But following the two wide spread up candles weakness then appears, but this is supported with further buying, and on up we go to the top of the rally and into old congestion areas.

Not a simple example, and far from straightforward, but one where the buying was clearly signaled with lower uncertainty on the trade as a result.

My Notes

USD/NOK - 15 minute

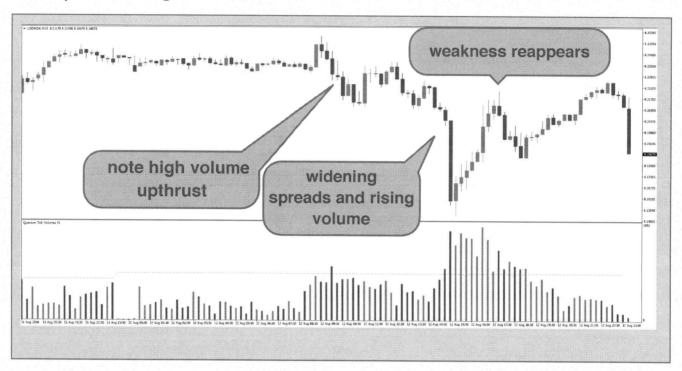

Back to calmer waters...and oil! And this is a super example of many different aspects of volume price analysis in action.

First of all let's start with the congestion phase on the left of the chart. Here we see the classic relationship between price and volume in this phase.

The market is waiting, and the spreads are narrow and moving in a very tight range, with the volume in agreement throughout, as it is well below average. This is what we expect to see.

The market makers are sitting on the sidelines here. They are not playing tricks, but simply watching and waiting, and no doubt preparing their next campaign.

Then we see a possible break to the up side with an increase in volume, but this looks weak as the selling knocks it back with no clear close above resistance. Note the high volume on the upthrust as the market falls and tests this region.

There is a further attempt to rally on the wide spread up candle, but the volume is relatively low, and indeed marginally lower than the previous attempt to rise, so with no follow through the pair rolls over again.

And note the falling volume into each rally, it is getting weaker and weaker. Then the pair begins to break below the support region, and gather momentum on rising volume, all classic signals.

The market makers then move in to buy on the up candles, but look at the effort to rise - enormous volume, wicks, and narrow spreads. Weakness reappears as a result with the upthrust atop on high volume.

The two candle reversal off the low does see the market recover, but on falling volume into the end of the session.

USD/SEK - 15 minute

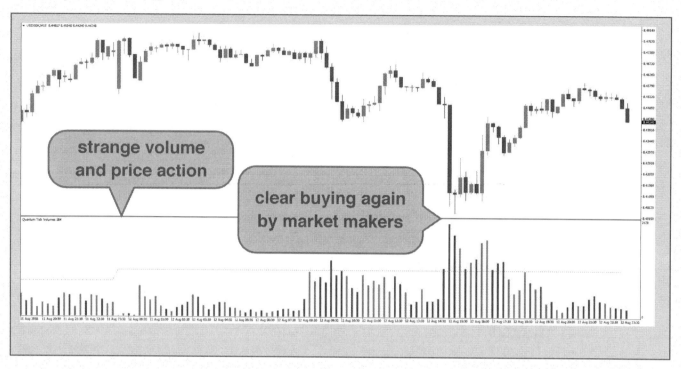

Another exotic currency pair, and an example of the candles and price action that can appear on such a pair.

The first to note is the strange price action to the left of the chart, and in particular the gapped down up candle on very low volume.

The subsequent candles are also unusual in that the volume is hardly visible, with volumes only returning to more 'normal' levels in the ensuing congestion phase.

The remainder of the price action is very similar to the previous chart for the USD/NOK, so I won't cover this in detail.

Only to say that once again the buying was clearer on the hammer candle at the base of the price waterfall.

If you are trading these pairs, you will find such price action occurring from time to time so don't be surprised.

These are volatile and often illiquid pairs, with gaps both up and down as the price action often does not flow immediately from open to close.

Volume still holds true with such pairs, but with thinner liquidity can be more spiky and in some ways is similar to the price action and volume associated with penny stocks or pink sheet stocks, or the less heavily traded futures contracts.

Bitcoin futures would be one topical example where price action can be spiky with gaps and sudden changes in volume.

USD/ZAR - 15 minute

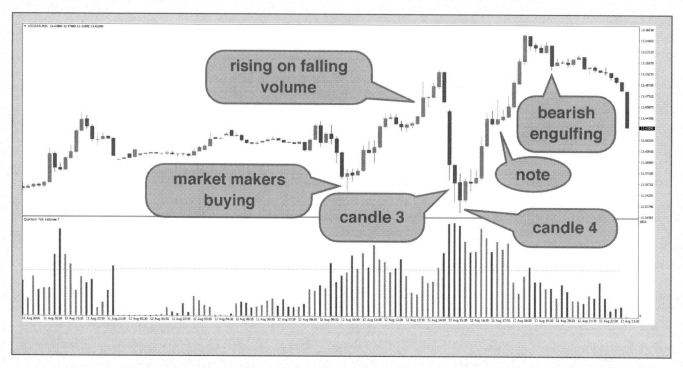

Once again we have volatile price action, this time with the South African Rand. This is another of the exotic currency pairs, but a popular one nevertheless given its association with the price of gold, and one that is increasingly available on the MT4 platform.

However, like many other currency pairs of this type, the pair is subject to volatility, and hot money flows chasing yield, which is great if you are on the right side, but not so good if you are caught out on the wrong side of any position.

We have some excellent price action after the move lower at the end of the congestion phase, as market maker buying appears on good volume with the hammer and narrow spread candles before the rally starts, and rises firmly, but on falling volume.

Note at the top of the rally we have a bearish engulfing candle which, like the two bar reversal, is often associated with a reversal in trend, as is the case here.

But what is interesting here in the move lower are the four down candles.

First we have the bearish engulfing candle, on above average volume. Then we see three down candles where the volume is almost identical on each. This sends us a very clear and unequivocal signal the market makers are buying here. Why? Because for the same effort we should expect to see the same result, according to Wyckoff's third law.

But we are not seeing this on candles three and four. In both cases the spreads have narrowed dramatically, and this can only mean one thing.

The market makers have moved in to buy with stopping volume, and so it proves, with the pair rising strongly on very supportive volume. However, note the up candle in this sequence with the deep wick. Selling pressure is entering the market and making life difficult for the insiders.

The bearish engulfing candle signals the end of the rally, following a weak up candle.

Section Four - 5 minute charts

In this section we move to the five minute timeframe, and here the issue of the comparative nature of volume at the crossover periods becomes less of an issue.

Because once the first three or four candle have been built, we then have a very good benchmark for our volume in the new session, so it's more straightforward.

The five minute chart is also an excellent timeframe for learning to apply volume price analysis at the live edge of the market. It is the perfect timeframe - not too fast and not too slow, and is a great way to learn.

And whilst you can choose any pair to do this, I would suggest some of the more even paced majors such as the USD/CAD, the AUD/USD and the GBP/USD (once the Brexit brouhaha has calmed).

These are excellent pairs, and any demo account with MT4 or any other platform gives you the tools you need - just volume and price.

Worked Examples

AUD/CAD - 5 minute

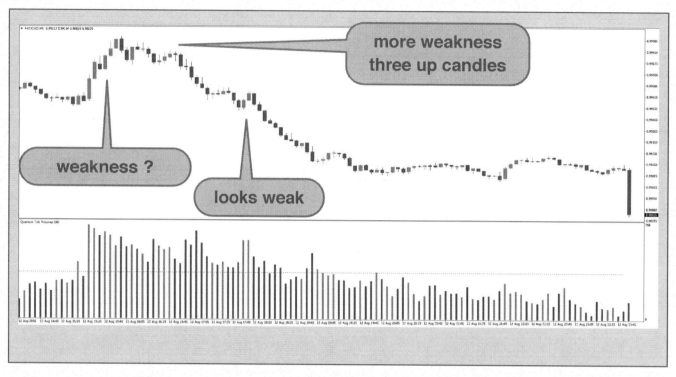

And so to an even faster timeframe, and here I have put together a collection from the 5 minute charts. The principles however are exactly the same, as I'm sure you appreciate.

We start at the left of the chart with a strong move away from congestion with the market makers participating on very high volume.

The first two candles are in agreement with high volume and solid price action, and no wicks to the top of either candle. But the next candle suggests some weakness. More volume arrives on the subsequent candle with further weakness on the candle with the wick to the top.

Finally at the top we have a two bar reversal, which immediately reverses the pair to the down-side.

We then see some further weakness on high volume, but no advancement in price. There is a small move lower, and yet more weakness on the three up candles, one after the other, and all on high volume, very narrow spreads to the body, and with wicks to the upper body.

This is certainly not a sign of strength, and a reverse is building here.

Then the bearish trend starts to pick up momentum on rising volume.

Congestion follows with two up candles on very high volume, and for comparison we only need to look to the left of the chart and the volume associated with the initial rally higher.

Here we had a wide spread in price, yet here with only slightly less volume we have a narrow spread of price. This signals more weakness ahead.

The market makers are selling into weakness in preparation for the next phase lower, with the bearish engulfing candle on the second of these signaling the re-establishment of the primary trend lower once more.

AUD/CHF - 5 minute

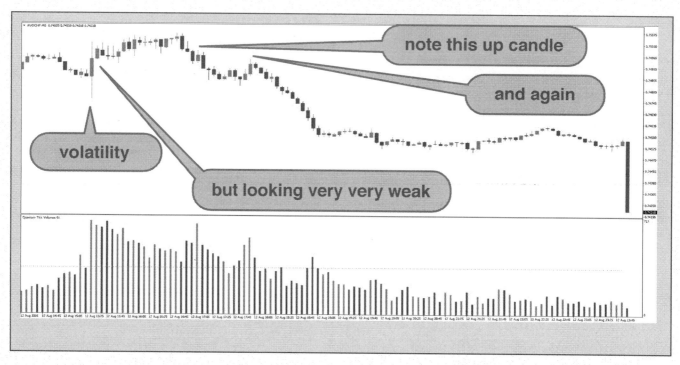

The sequence here starts with volatility to the left of the chart, and as usual all we can gauge from this price action is we have participation by the market makers given the associated volume.

The pair then moves higher, but this looks very, very weak.

First we have a series of shooting stars on ultra high volume followed by further high volume, but which fails to take the market higher.

The market makers are driving volume into the market here and selling with no response higher, and so we can assume the market makers are distributing here in the selling climax, and away we go.

Note the narrow spread up candle as the downtrend begins on ultra high volume. This is a sure sign of weakness, and confirms what we have already seen in the selling climax.

This is repeated once again on the two candle rally as the volume rises. However, we are now well below the ceiling of resistance, so any move higher will need to see significant effort if the pair is to advance further.

The waterfall then begins to develop, and as it does the spreads begin to widen with the volumes rising, before the pair moves into the congestion phase as the volume fades.

And as always it is important to remember the volume on the second half of the chart is compressed, because of the volume in the first half. Extreme volumes will always impact volume both before and after, and it is important to remember this at all times.

In the price waterfall for example, it would be easy to conclude that volume is relatively low. And here the word relative is all important, as it is relative to the extreme volume of earlier. So in the context of volume it would be high, if the extreme volume were not on the chart.

AUD/JPY - 5 minute

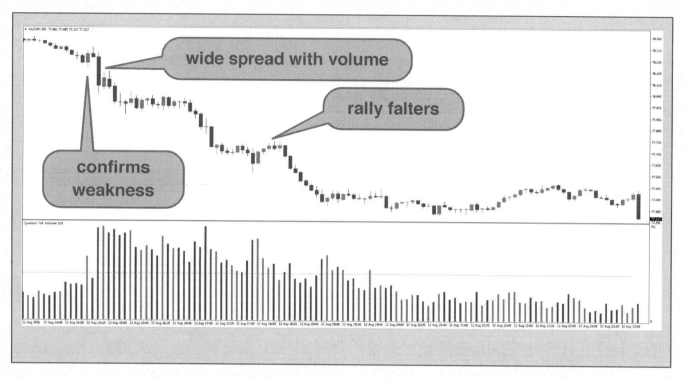

This is another classic price chart where we have the waterfall developing, then pausing into congestion, before developing once again, and moving down into the next level.

And of course this pair is a barometer of market sentiment and risk given the risk currency on one side, and the safe haven currency on the other.

But if we start at the top left of the chart, the initial move lower is stately, after which we see an injection of volume on a narrow spread up candle, which signals more weakness to come as the market makers begin selling here more strongly.

This is followed by another weak candle.

Then we receive the first wide spread down candle on high volume with the subsequent candle delivering a firm signal of weakness, as it is a narrow spread up candle on even higher volume, which is then repeated.

And down we go to the next level.

Now we have extended price action in the congestion phase. A solid floor and ceiling are built here, which once breached confirms the ongoing weakness, and down we go on rising volume, and into a further congestion phase, which is not so tightly defined as the first.

Note the two bar reversal on high volume, but then the rally falters with falling volume and a rising market on narrowing spreads, telling us there is weakness ahead.

And down we go to the final phase. This is classic 'stepped' price action. Not all waterfalls are dramatic. This is one of the more stately ones, punctuated with both congestion periods and trends.

AUD/NZD - 5 minute

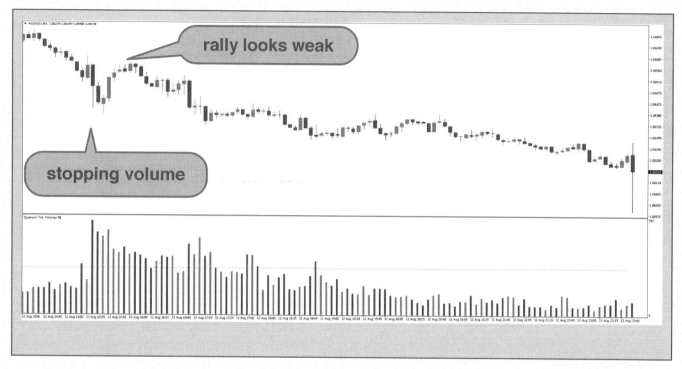

Another example of a stately move lower for the Aussie dollar, this time against its near neighbor the New Zealand dollar.

As we begin from the left of the chart, the initial waterfall develops nicely, and remember the volume bars would have been taller prior to the arrival of the market makers.

Then they step in on the down candle with volume, but one which develops a deep wick to the lower body. This is the highest volume of the session, and is most definitely stopping volume here.

The market makers have decided to buy here, to stop the price falling further, with the deep wick to the lower body of the candle and ultra high volume, confirming this fact.

The next candle is also down, but has no wicks and is on high volume, but sits inside the spread of the previous candle so bearish selling pressure appears to be waning, before further buying appears on the narrow spread up candle, and up we go.

However, the rally looks weak.

The first candle in the sequence looks good. It is a nice wide spread up candle with excellent volume, so no signals here.

The two candles that follow are very different, and signal weakness ahead. Volume is high and yet the spreads are very narrow, and confirmed by the third candle in this sequence. The spreads are narrowing, and the volume is high but falling.

Such volume should be driving the market much higher and faster. It is not because the market makers are selling into weakness.

The volume action gradually subsides away as the price action slides lower. Some currency cross pairs exhibit this gradual price action, but generally moves to the downside are typically much faster.

And this was also towards the end of the session and week so everyone was squaring positions, and closing ahead of the weekend.

AUD/USD - 5 minute

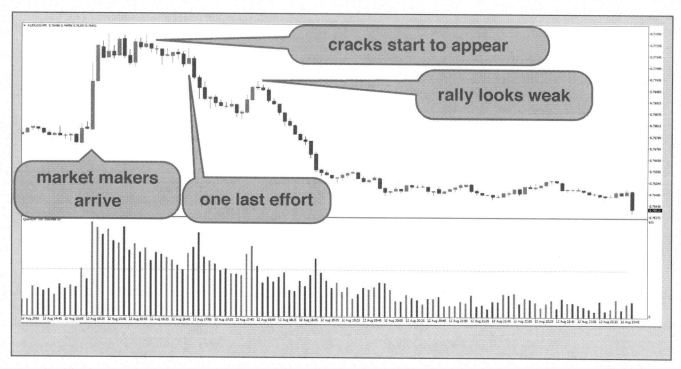

This is a more typical price waterfall with the Aussie dollar.

The initial entrance of the market makers looks strong. Two wide spread up candles on very high volume. There appears to be little weakness at this point, other than on the first of these, where we have some evidence of selling as we have a wick to the top of the candle.

However, it is not well developed, and at this point more characteristic of early profit taking. And the second candle rings no alarm bells.

The next candle is down, and is a narrow spread candle on high volume, so there is some selling. This is often the case, and is simply profit taking again after such a strong move. But then the cracks start to appear.

First we have an upthrust candle on very high volume and the selling by the market makers starts.

There then follows a smaller example, as the market makers continue to sell. Then comes a two bar reversal. Further weakness signals follow, with the market makers pushing the prices higher and selling into weakness.

There is one last effort on the upthrust candle, and the market breaks lower on rising volume before it falls, after which the price flattens into congestion, and we have a rally.

The two up candles in the rally look fine, before weakness appears once again with the small candle at the top which is on average volume with selling volumes then building once again, and the pair moves down into the long congestion phase at the bottom as volume dies away.

CAD/JPY - 5 minute

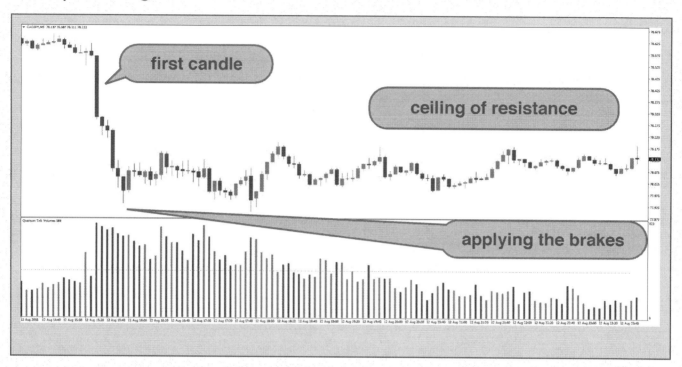

This was almost certainly a move triggered by a news release or item of economic data, or could even have been oil related. The market moves rapidly here, and is exactly what the market makers enjoy.

There are no major pause points here, and no stopping to sell back into weakness. If you were not short before, this is a tricky position to enter, as there are no 'confidence building' candles here to offer that low risk entry. It is just a fact of trading life that sometimes they simply do not appear.

The first candle has no wicks, but high volume. This is just pure selling here, and a strong signal on its own. Because if there were any wicks at all, this might suggest profit taking or market maker buying. But there are none here, it is just a clean candle from top to bottom.

The next is narrower as the market makers are selling into the waterfall, and the same again in the next candle. Then on down into another wide spread candle on high volume, before they move in once again to begin the stopping process, and apply the brakes with the two bar reversal on high volume.

From here we develop into the classic price action of the buying climax as the pair is whipsawed around on both high and reduced volume. This is the classic price action of the climax, as the market makers move the pair back and forth to shake out further sellers. You can think of this as the ripples on the pond.

The explosive move is the large stone landing in the pond or lake, and the waves created are instant and large, but gradually die away as they move further from the landing point. It is the same here.

The initial shock waves are large, but as the mopping up phases develops, both volume and the price action calm.

EUR/AUD - 5 minute

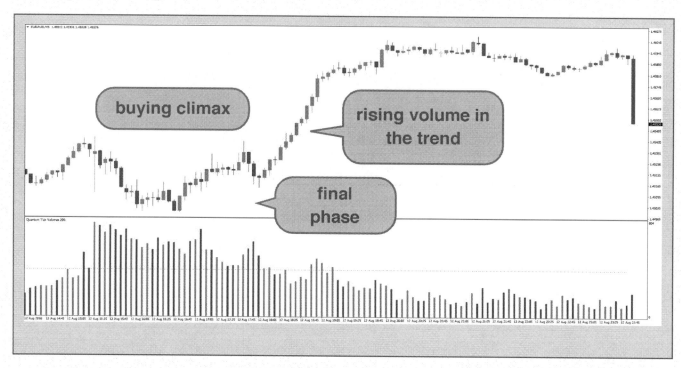

Once again on this chart we have a classic example of accumulation in the buying climax on a five minute timeframe. Remember, these occur in all timeframes, and are not the sole province of the slower timeframes. On a fast chart such as this, it is possible to see a complete cycle from the selling climax to the buying climax and back again within a few hours.

It is all relative to the timeframe under consideration. All price action is self similar, and repeats across the timeframes. It is wheels within wheels, or the Russian doll analogy.

And again, this is very typical of the volume and related price action you are likely to see. The whipsaw price action and volume is driven in, with traders buying into a move, but then selling in panic as more traders are encouraged to buy, and then selling again, as the price action is pushed higher and lower.

There is a whole variety of buying and selling within the price action.

The final phase of the buying climax is confirmed by the three down candles, before the trend higher begins on below average volume, but then builds slowly as the trend gathers momentum higher, before finally dwindling away as we move into the congestion phase at the top of the chart.

Note that in the uptrend we have generally rising volume, and it is only when we reach the congestion phase, do we start to see some anomalies once more.

The climatic volume here is very typical, and something that will appear across any timeframe. This could be a monthly chart for a stock for example, or as here on a 5 minute currency pair. The purpose is the same. The accumulation phase is underway, and a campaign is being prepared.

Note too there was no test here prior to the rally higher. The insiders do not use tests all the time, but when they appear are good signals to see.

EUR/CAD - 5 minute

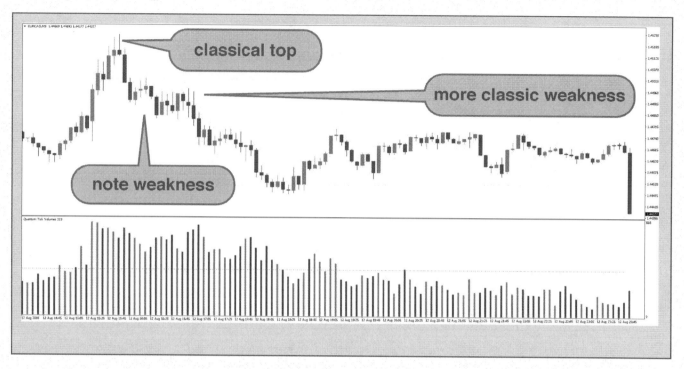

Some even paced price action here with volume describing each and every move.

If we begin to the immediate left of the chart, the initial move lower is on average volume for the first few candles with supportive buying, before the trend develops on rising volume driving the pair higher.

Once again, remember these volume bars would have been taller and more descriptive prior to the market makers moving in, and increasing the volume dramatically. The trend higher then begins, and is given an injection of momentum and volume as the market makers move in.

We then reach the top with volume remaining at extreme levels, where the price action is topped off with a doji candle followed by a classic upthrust or shooting star. The doji candle is indecisive, but the shooting star on very high volume tells its own story.

Selling by the market makers then begins in earnest.

Note the weakness of the attempt to rally following the first two wide spread down candles, and once again the final up candle of these three is another with a deep wick to the top on high volume, and a great entry point, or confidence builder in an existing short position.

A further congestion phase then builds before we see the classic down candle with the wick to the top of the body.

This is the deep wick candle on high volume, followed by the next on higher volume still, before we move into another pause and congestion phase with volume remaining high, and further weakness evident with the wicks and price spreads telling their own story.

Finally, we reach a bottom as selling pressure from the market makers subsides, and we move into an extended congestion phase as the next campaign is prepared.

EUR/CHF - 5 minute

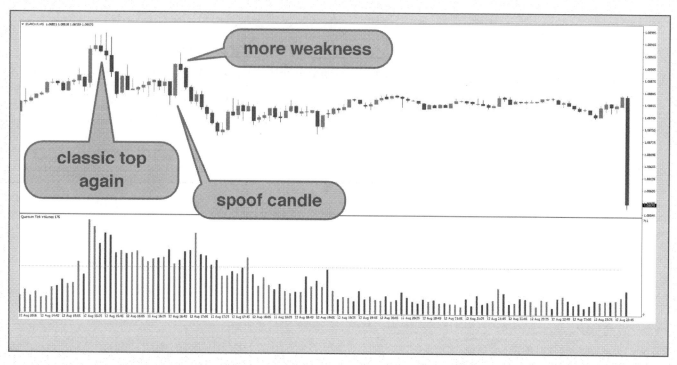

Some more great price action here.

And if we start at the left of the chart, where congestion had been building. Then the market makers inject volume on the wide spread up candle, and which is also the highest volume of the period.

But look at the next candle, and one that should make you tingle in anticipation. It has identical volume, but there is no follow through.

The market makers are selling heavily. And twice more, with one final heave upwards for luck before driving the pair lower on high volume.

When these sorts of candles appear on such volume, the outcome is almost guaranteed, and it is only a question of time before the move lower commences. So it is not a question of if, but when, and all that's required is patience.

In this example we have three candles sending the same message. The market makers are selling, and selling heavily here. The price action alone tells us the market is weak. The volume confirms it.

And the fact that all three have failed to breach the same price level, adds further weight, if indeed any further weight were needed.

Then down we go into the congestion phase with a spoof candle higher on average volume. Why is it a spoof? Well, the price action is the same as the wide spread up candle on the break higher.

So identical price action, but the volume on the second is half the volume of the first. A simple analysis, but so powerful.

More downside momentum follows, and note the attempt to rally with the high volume bar and narrow spread candle. A clear signal again of more weakness to come.

EUR/GBP - 5 minute

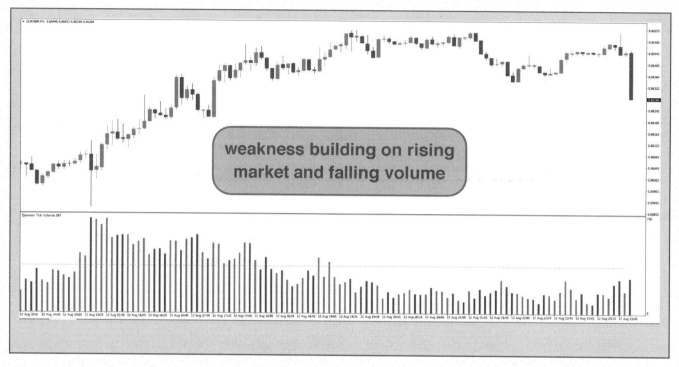

This is almost a perfect example of the 'longer term' relationship between volume and price. In other words, a rising market and falling volume can only be weak, and this chart really frames this concept over a broader horizon.

Yes, we do see this on groups of candles as we have seen over the examples in the book, but this is a great example of 'stepping back' from the close analysis of each candle and volume bar, and seeing the bigger picture.

In fact in many ways, this is also a perfect mirror image with one reflecting the other.

All the components are here, of rallies, of buying of support and of selling, but when played out in the context of the chart, they also describe why the congestion phase has arrived, with the volumes continuing to fall as we move into this phase of price action.

The final candle is not significant here, and was simply reflecting the end of the session and rollover.

As volume traders we do focus a great deal on the detail, but remember to step back occasionally and cast your eye over the entire chart in order to get a sense of the broad trend and the volume profiles.

My Notes

EUR/NZD - 5 minute

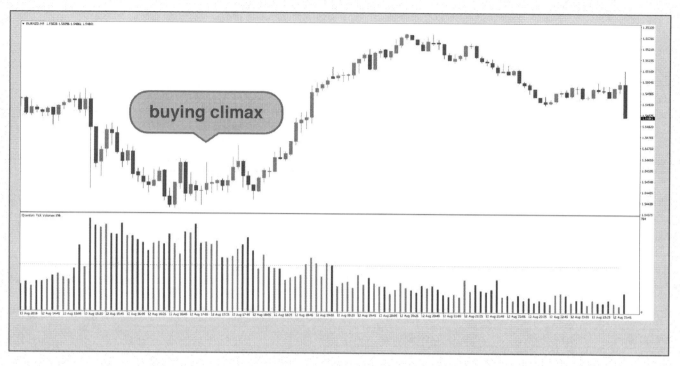

Another great example of the buying climax, but also one which demonstrates a further facet of volume price analysis, which is simply to be patient and not jump in too early.

Starting at the left of the chart, the initial candle of interest is clear, and is the deep wick down candle on ultra high volume. At that point we might become very excited, and it would be easy to jump in immediately, and buy on the signal.

But then the market moves lower, and into the typical whipsaw price action of buying and selling, as the market makers push and pull the price action, driving it this way and that in order to accumulate further, and remove the selling pressure before starting the campaign higher.

There are no hard and fast rules here. Sometimes the trend will develop quickly, but most times it will not, so the congestion phase follows.

Here we have the 'overrun' aspect of the initial signal, and perhaps the takeaway here is that the candle is 'extreme' and unusual. Normally we would look for a more 'considered' hammer candle so perhaps this was a heads up warning in itself?

When you see a candle such as this, just wait and treat it with caution. So the question here is, at what point might we consider entering such a move? And there are two answers here.

First when the price action and volume gives us the confidence to enter.

The second is once any areas of resistance have been taken out, and so offer a strong platform of support. Which is where we turn to classic price based support and resistance levels for help, and which are also part of volume price analysis.

This is all explained in detail in my book A Complete Guide To Volume Price Analysis.

EUR/USD - 5 minute

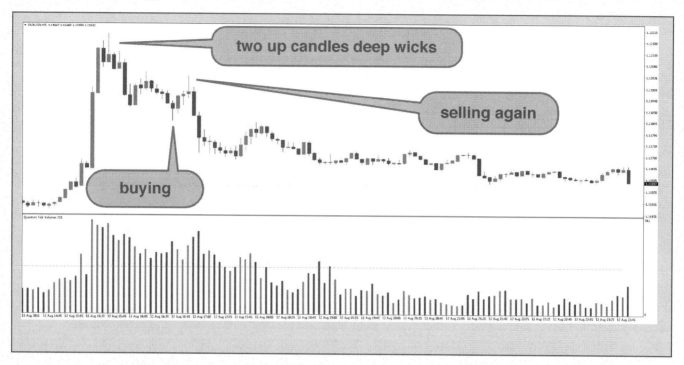

Some sumptuous price action here, and one where you would be spoilt for choice in terms of getting in, which would only depend on your risk appetite. In other words, get in at the top, the next level down, or even on the third or fourth rally? The choice is yours as the signals are all there.

After the initial surge, weakness is heralded by two candles with deep wicks on high volume before the pair rolls over, and into the next phase.

There is more weakness with a further fall before the market makers step in to buy, selling into the weakness again before moving on down to the next level. Note the wonderful shooting star candle as the precursor to this move lower, and once again a powerful signal, and perfect entry point if you missed out earlier.

Finally we move down, and into the congestion phases with some minor rallies and falls.

And remember the euro dollar is the most heavily traded pair in the forex market with the tightest spreads, so getting in is easy, with volume price analysis then helping you to stay in to maximise profits.

My Notes

GBP/AUD - 5 minute

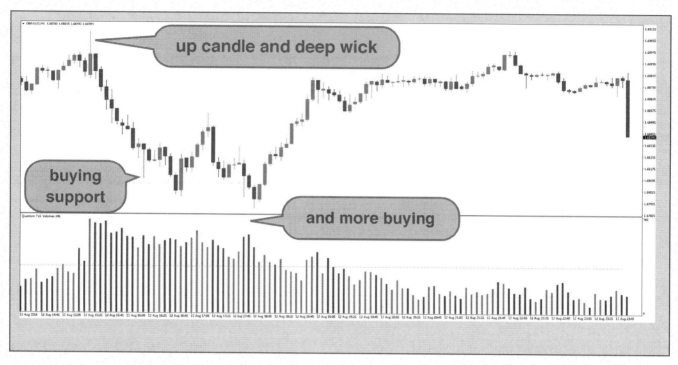

I have included this example as it is one where we did indeed have a 'single candle signal' to start the firing gun of the campaign.

As I said before, there are no hard and fast rules and we have to use our judgement, and here the move was fast.

The entry of the market makers is denoted by the up candle and deep wick to the upper body, which is a clear sign of weakness.

The market makers have moved in and sold heavily into weakness, and the subsequent price waterfall then develops very quickly.

Note the initial buying which appears on the down candle with the deep wick two thirds of the way down, before continuing lower, and reversing on the bullish engulfing candle, and up into the rally, which is once again topped off by....... a shooting star candle on extreme volume.

So we know this rally is not going far, and the market makers are selling heavily here.

And then down again into a further buying phase.

The campaign higher is then prepared, and moved firmly away on good volume and into the congestion phase as volume dwindles away.

Please note the last candle on the chart is the end of the week and session close, coupled with rollover.

GBP/CAD - 5 minute

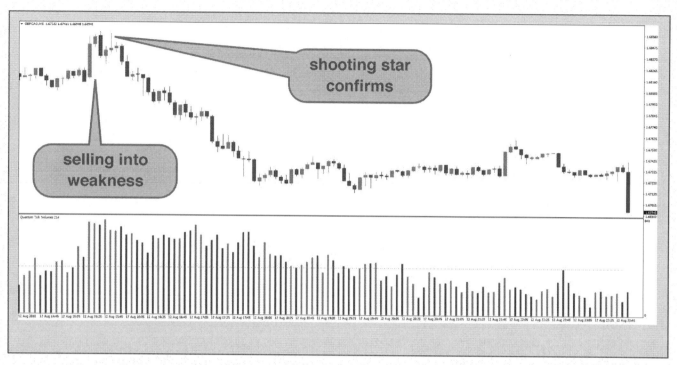

In this example we move back to consider the finer detail of the charts with the market initially in congestion, before the volume rises dramatically on the first wide spread up candle and moves higher.

Then comes the second candle, which has a narrow spread on identical volume as the first, and this can only mean one thing. The market makers are selling out strongly here, which is duly confirmed with the bearish engulfing candle on very high volume.

The minor rally comes to a halt, with the shooting star candle validating the weakness at this level, and in addition creating the ceiling of resistance.

A further tiny candle then appears on very high volume telling us the market is now fragile, and ready to break, and away we go.

What is interesting on this chart are the intermediate congestion phases, as there are no very clear signals prior to the next break lower developing, so it is a little harder to jump into the trend on this one.

But as we move lower and down to the next congestion phase, they are most certainly there with narrow spreads and high volume, and very clear anomalies that are hard to miss.

The clearest signal however comes right at the top on the ultra high volume, and would have been the place to enter, with a wide stop loss to allow for any continued attempts to rally.

Getting into a trend early at a reversal point always carries more risk, and this is reflected in the fact you will need to set any stop loss that much wider as you cannot be sure how long the market will remain at this level, before moving, and may even attempt to rally several times.

But, the payoff is you are in the trend earlier.

Trading is all about risk and reward. In this set up you are taking a little more risk, but are rewarded with more of the trend. Join lower, and the stop loss is closer, but you have less of the trend to take out.

It is all about risk and reward, which in essence is all the financial markets are about. Risk on reflects higher risk for higher reward, whilst risk off, reflects the opposite.

GBP/CHF - 5 minute

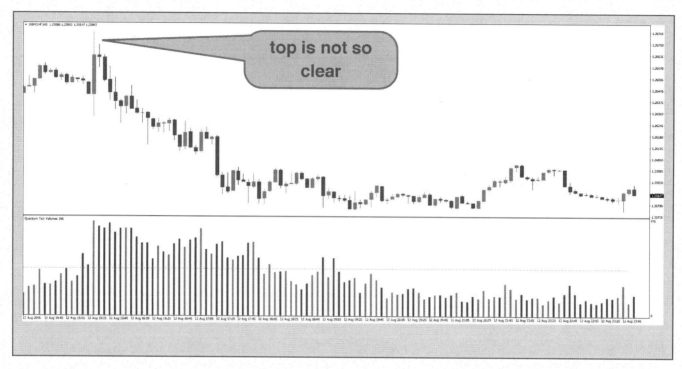

And this is an example where the extreme top is not so clear.

The initial candle is tricky to analyze. It is similar to a doji candle, and from the price action it is very hard to decide whether it is a sign of strength or weakness. We have wicks to top and bottom as well as a wide body. And at times like this I would suggest two things.

First patience. If you are not sure, don't guess. Wait for clearer signals to appear.

Second, move to other timeframes as this may well help to 'disassemble' the candle into five one minute candles, or give you a longer term perspective say on the 15 minute chart for example.

This can often be a great help in clarifying such price action, and of course will also give you an alternative perspective. Using a multi timeframe approach is a key part of any trading approach, and here it helps to provide an alternative view of the price action, when the one you are considering is not clear

I cannot recommend this too strongly.

You will no doubt have multiple timeframes anyway, but when one such candle arrives - move to another timeframe for further clarification.

My Notes

GBP/NZD - 5 minute

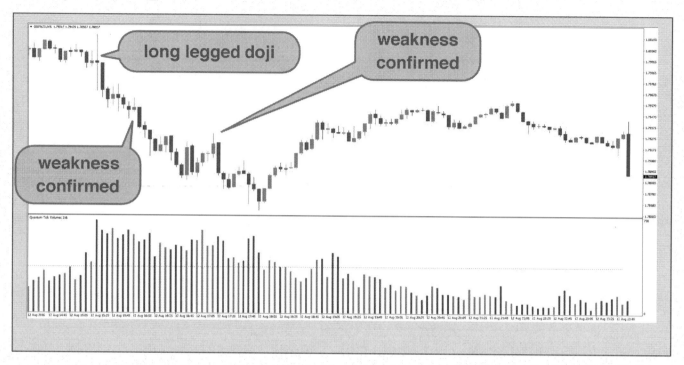

Once again this is the same period of price action in a sterling related pair, where the start of the trend is far from clear.

On this occasion we have a very distinctive long legged doji associated with ultra high volume, so all we can assume here is the market makers are in the market buying and selling on the volatility.

We can make no conclusion here on the proposed direction for the campaign, so have to be patient.

Do not assume such a candle is indicative of a change in trend - it is not. Step one is to analyze the candle in a faster timeframe.

The wide spread down candle that follows then confirms the bearish sentiment, and is also on very high volume so clearly there is selling here, but until the candle has cleared the lower leg of the doji candle, it might be prudent to wait.

The pause point in the move lower is punctuated with further doji candles, and it is not until the upthrust candle appears prior to an exit into the next phase, and is on very high volume, do we have a more straightforward entry.

And indeed at the next rally we see a repeat with another clear signal of further weakness as the candle closes with a deep upper wick and high volume.

Then down we go to the buying as the market makers step back in, and off we go to the upside, but on gently falling volume.

So the rally looks weak and is unlikely to go far.

GBP/USD - 5 minute

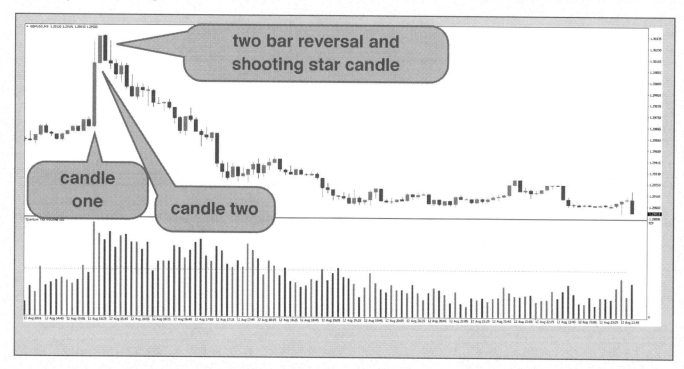

I have included this chart for the Cable, as it gives us another perspective on the start of the trend.

As we have already seen from earlier examples, sentiment for the British pound in this timeframe was universally bearish, so giving us an excellent confirming signal when entering positions, with one chart validating another. This is not always the case, but is a helpful aspect to consider.

The first wide spread up candle appears on ultra high volume, but has a deep wick to the upper body, so whilst the initial response is bullish, the wick reveals the depth of selling in the candle. Then we have a second candle with high volume, and no wicks.

And it would be very easy at this point to jump on the trend as there is nothing to suggest the reversal that is about to happen.

So what is the answer here? And this is one where one other technical tool will come to our aid which are part of volume price analysis, and that is support and resistance.

Always check for such levels once a move begins as they will help to build confidence in entry and exit and also answer the question, 'why'?

The next candle makes the position very clear, but by then we may have already entered on the second candle. So always check other technical aspects of the charts before jumping in.

Once in train, the trend is easy to pick up and the clue here was threefold.

First, selling in candle one with the deep wick to the candle. Second, the marginal close above the high of candle one. In other words the price is struggling to move outside the range of the first candle.

Third, the spread on candle two was less than half that of candle one on the same volume, so clearly an anomaly in terms of effort and result.

NZD/CAD - 5 minute

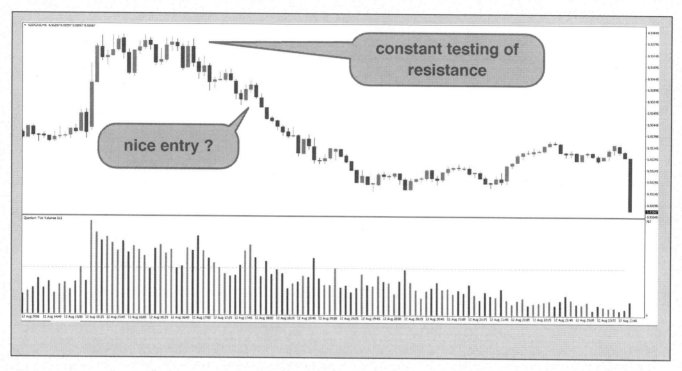

And purely by coincidence we have a similar set up here. This time though we have a more extended phase of price action before the trend breaks lower, and a wonderful example of the building of resistance which holds throughout.

Again we have two wide spread up candles to start the move. Traders are dragged in on the fear of missing out. The first has the wick, and the second follows through, but unlike the previous example, the spreads of the two candles are more alike, and so there is little or no anomaly here.

Then weakness appears on the down candle following these two. The pair has attempted to rise, but closed below the open, and so created the wick to the upper body on good volume.

This initial sign of weakness is further confirmed two candles later with another - this time it's an up candle, and one with a narrow body and deep wick to the upper body.

And here I would like to stress support and resistance once again, and reinforce my comments from the previous example.

Here we have high volume with constant testing and retesting of the price area above on ten separate occasions, but it is never breached. This alone is enough to signal weakness. Equally the floor of support is substantial.

As this region is building we cannot be certain which way the campaign will move. Patience is therefore required when trading a break away opportunity.

And indeed as the floor of support is finally breached, note the volume on the candle. This is a genuine move, not a fake move or a trap. The ceiling of resistance is then retested. This is often the case, before the move picks up momentum.

Once it breaks we can join the move lower, and note the two up candles on the second rally on high volume and narrow spreads. A nice entry point perhaps?

USD/CAD - 5 minute

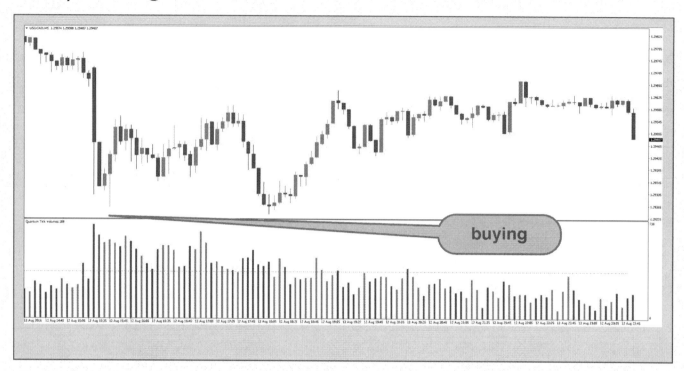

Another tricky one to read here with the USD/CAD, and this time to the short side.

Here the market has been trending lower so we are perhaps expecting a strong move to the downside. The first candle is formed as the market makers inject both momentum and volatility, but note the wick to the bottom of the candle. There is sustained buying here.

The second candle then forms on the same volume and completes within the spread of the first candle, meaning the low of the first candle has not been taken out.

Then an up candle appears on high volume, followed by a deep wick up candle which drives the market higher. There then follows some very choppy price action, and the reason here was a series of news releases with US, Canadian and then oil data all playing a part in the associated price action.

So plenty of opportunity for the market makers to move the market this way and that on a constant stream of news.

And at times like this it is often best to stay out of such a pair and look for other markets and opportunities, which will be more straightforward than this one.

USD/JPY - 5 minute

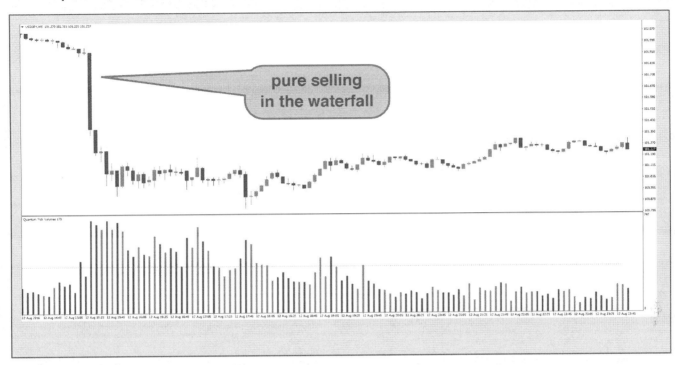

A very rapid move here, and once again one that is preceded with bearish sentiment, before the market makers move in with ultra high volume on the initial candle.

As there are no wicks here the selling pressure is pure and clear.

Once again, a very strong signal of a continuation of the move. The second candle then builds, but is perhaps a signal the heavy selling of the first candle is now over extended. The second candle has a relatively small spread, but on the same volume.

Nevertheless the move lower continues with a repeat, and on down again on high volume with a two bar reversal as it hits the bottom.

The congestion phase then builds, and note the efforts to rally with the high volume up candles, as they build a channel of resistance and support accordingly.

This is finally breached, but there is no follow through and immediately buying enters, and a gentle rally higher ensues.

The volume then starts to dwindle away as the congestion phase extends to the end of the session.

USD/MXN - 5 minute

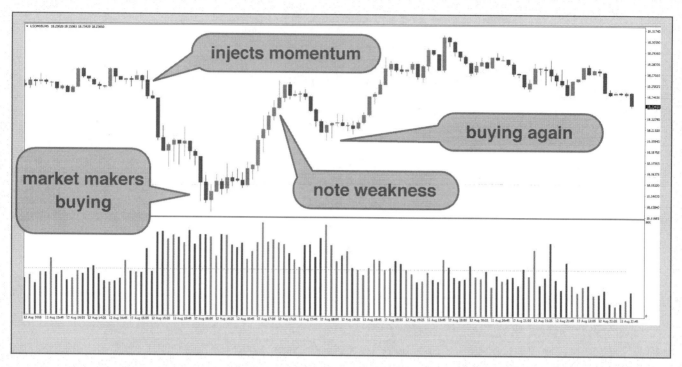

And here we return to the exotic pairs, and as always with such currency pairs, we need to be on our toes all the time. The trends are there, but they do reverse quickly, so we can't afford to over-stay our welcome!

A nice solid period of congestion builds initially to the left of the chart, and then the move begins with the trend lower. The initial candle here is one of my personal favorites. It has a wick to the top, and the spread of the candle takes out the floor of support.

This sort of candle always seems to inject momentum. The effect I believe is from the initial move higher, and then the reversal into the down body. This type of candle is like the 'last hurrah'. In other words, one last effort before the market gives up and the move develops.

The only analogy I can think of here, is of a ballon filling with water, with the weight of water in the ballon adding increasing weight, before it finally bursts and the move begins.

Then we are off, down to the secondary level, and finally down to the accumulation where buying arrives on high volume, with the wick to the wide spread down candle signaling the start of this phase, and followed by further buying.

Then the trend higher begins on rising volume, but note the weakness that appears as we reach the pause point with the deep wick to the candle on good volume.

The pair moves lower, but we see further buying from the market makers, first on the narrow spread up candle on extreme volume, and repeated with the hammer candle on high volume.

This is sufficient to take us up to the next level, and into the final congestion phase of the session on good volume. At this point support and resistance then become key as the next phase of the campaign gets underway.

USD/NOK - 5 minute

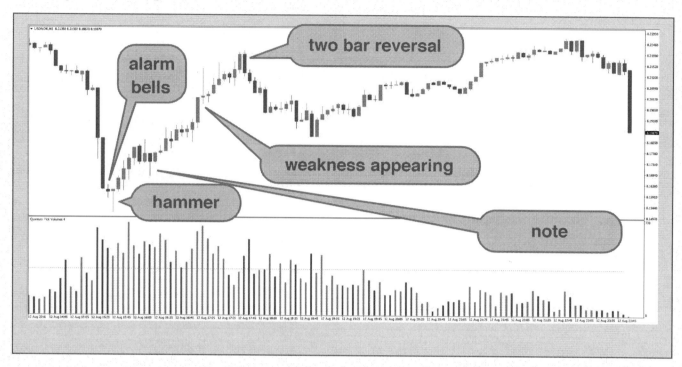

Some excellent price action here with the USD/NOK, and some very descriptive examples.

The initial move lower starts at the left of the chart with rising volume as the pair breaks below the support platform before pausing, and then breaking lower as the market makers drive prices lower quickly.

The first wide spread down candle looks fine, but with a wick to the lower body suggests some buying.

The second candle then delivers the follow through, but on slightly lower volume. Then the third down candle arrives, and the narrow spread sets the alarm bells ringing. It is very narrow, and yet the volume remains high.

If ever there was an anomaly this has to be it!

This is then followed by a hammer on high volume, and we see a rare 'V shaped rally' develop, which do happen. Under normal circumstances we would expect to see congestion after such a rapid move, but not on this occasion as the market makers move in strongly.

Note the market maker buying at the first pause point, and then we are off to the next level with price rising on rising volume.

Then we see the first signs of weakness with the upthrust candle on ultra high volume followed by another at a higher level, before the trend tops out on a two bar reversal, and moves back lower on rising volume.

Finally, we move back higher to complete the session.

A great example of how being light on your feet, and reading the clues and signals delivered by volume price analysis would have offered up some excellent trading opportunities.

USD/ZAR - 5 minute

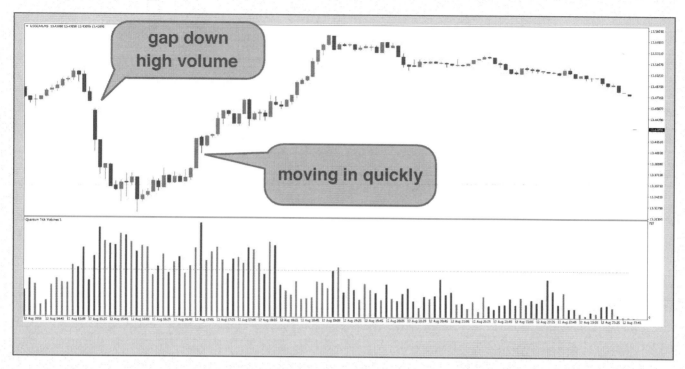

And finally to end this section with another exotic chart and examples of two very solid trends.

The first breaks lower on rising volume, and note the gapped down candle on high volume confirming the heavy market maker selling at this point. Volume then increases on the next candle, before the first signs of buying appear with the small up candle, with a wick to the lower body.

However, the next candle is wide and down, before narrow spread candles appear on high volume as the market makers absorb the selling pressure, and prepare to reverse the trend.

The move through the resistance area created is strong with a wide spread up candle on high volume, and note the market makers moving into quickly to buy the weakness on the first pause with the down candle on ultra high volume.

From there the move develops strongly, with the final phases moving upwards on relatively low volume - a warning sign the move is coming to an end, which indeed it duly does, and tails off on low volume as the session comes to an end.

My Notes

Section 5 - 4 hour charts

In this section we look at some examples from the four hour chart for spot forex.

And you may think it odd I have added these at the end given all the other timeframes are in chronological order, but there is a reason. I wanted to include them at the end as they do require a slightly different mindset when using volume price analysis.

Many traders say you cannot use this timeframe as the volume profiles are always the same. In other words high in London and the US and low in Asia.

In a sense this is true, and as you saw earlier, we also have similar issues when considering the hourly charts, but I hope I have convinced you the methodology works perfectly well on this time-frame. When moving to the four hour chart we need to consider the comparative aspects of volume in more detail, and in particular compare one session to another, but of the same period.

The four hour chart is also an interesting one as we can break the 24 hour trading day up into either four hour or eight hour segments. So six sessions of four hours each. It's not perfect, but it does give a 'framework' to our analysis, and helps to divide the chart into the various timezones and liquidity sessions. And as I hope you will see, the four hour chart still has something to offer us as volume traders.

The key take away here is to remember there will generally be a lag from one session over into the next. So what happens in the London session on one bar, may follow through into the London session the following day or two or more days later.

It is almost as though there is a delayed reaction. When you think about this logically this is no great surprise as the focus constantly shifts from one currency to another as the sessions move with the 24 hour clock.

So focus on the euro and the British pound will be very high in London, less so in the US session, and of very little interest in Asia and the Far East. So this 'cyclical' focus is really what the four hour chart is constantly describing, which is why I left it until the end of the book.

It really does break the market up into the session phases of local price action, which is why you will see the 'delayed reaction' effect coming into play here.

I hope you will agree.

So here are several examples from the currency majors.

Worked
Examples

AUD/USD - 4 hour

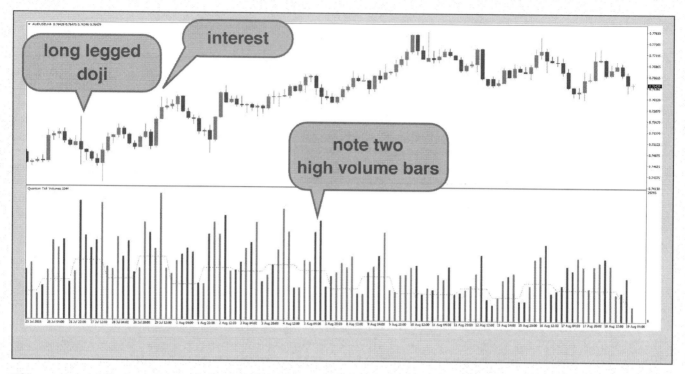

If we start with the Aussie dollar, and as I explained in the notes, we expect to see the cyclical rise and fall of the 24 hour trading day and which is as expected.

If we start on the left of the chart, the first visible signal is the long legged doji candle on high volume. No doubt this was a news release and volatility. High volume follows on narrow spread lows, before the deep wick candle appears on very high volume. The market makers are buying.

The next point of interest is the highest volume of the session on the up candle with the wick to the upper body.

Here the market makers are selling into weakness as the candle is topped with a wick. The pair failed to break any higher, and we see the delayed reaction as the market sells off before further buying arrives on the candle with the deep wick, with the pair rising over two candles on good volume.

Moving to the centre of chart note the two high volume bars as the market makers move in to buy, which delivered in the following sessions as the market trends higher.

And as we can see we are currently in an extended congestion phase with gently declining volume overall, and the pair is starting to look a little weak.

If the floor of support is breached on high session volume we can expect to see the Aussie dollar move into a bearish phase.

What this timeframe also provides is a more general view of volume over an extended period, which can often help to explain the longer term trend which then develops.

Here for example we can see the volume to the left of the chart is greater than that to the right. In other words, volume is declining over time, and if this were associated with a developed trend higher, then this might be signaling an exhaustion of the trend and possible reversal in the medium term.

This is perhaps more subtle, but these are the signals you need to consider for longer term trading.

EUR/USD - 4 hour

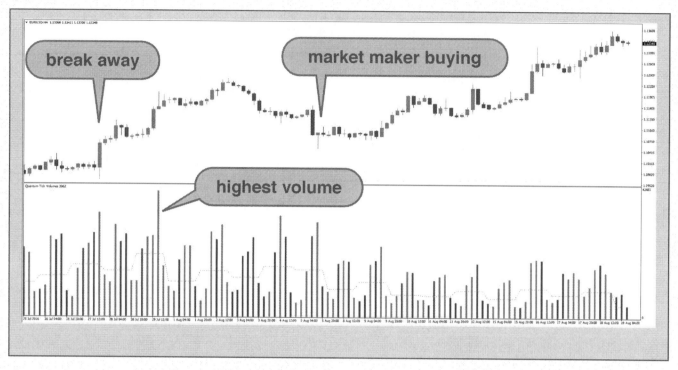

A neat example here of the four hour chart confirming a session break away, with the break away from congestion on session three on a high volume wide spread up candle, and duly followed with another.

Note the highest volume on the chart which appears under the shooting star candle, and signaling weakness ahead. But the reaction takes three or four sessions to materialize, and this is what I meant by the delayed reaction. On a one minute chart this would be seen in 15 or 20 minutes. On an hourly chart perhaps a day.

But here we are considering the impact over sessions. The pair does turn lower with the wide spread down candle accelerating progress, before the market makers step in again on the hammer candle and buy. Then we have congestion, and the delayed effect once more, before the pair begin the trend higher.

Note here also this chart is deep into the summer months so volumes are declining gently for seasonal reasons.

My Notes

GBP/USD - 4 hour

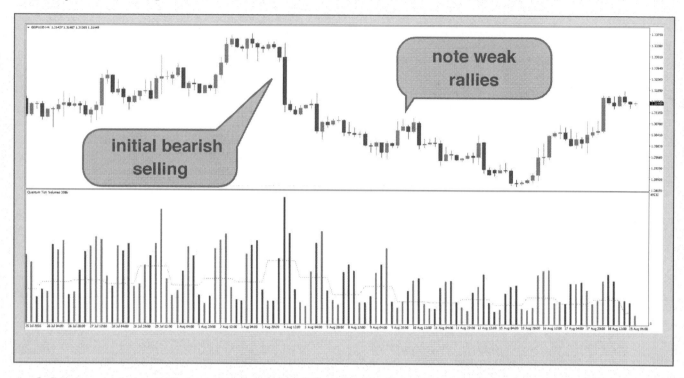

And this is another perfect example of the delayed reaction effect so typical of the four hour chart. Here we are with Cable, and in this case it is almost metronomic progress.

The initial bearish sentiment begins with a wide spread down candle on very high volume at the centre of the chart.

The market makers are selling heavily, and this is the highest volume on the chart. This sentiment then carries forward to the following session with a further wide spread down candle, before a weak attempt to rally on high volume fails to follow through.

More weakness ensues as we continue lower, and note the weak rallies particularly those on low volume.

And what is also interesting here is the general decline in the selling volumes on the down candles.

This is in part due to the seasonal aspect, but also reflects a general lack of selling pressure as the British pound continues to remain very oversold.

The gentle rally begins on above average volume, but with little sign of any significant accumulation here, we can expect to see a consolidation phase develop with the development of a buying climax perhaps into the later part of the year.

NZD/USD - 4 hour

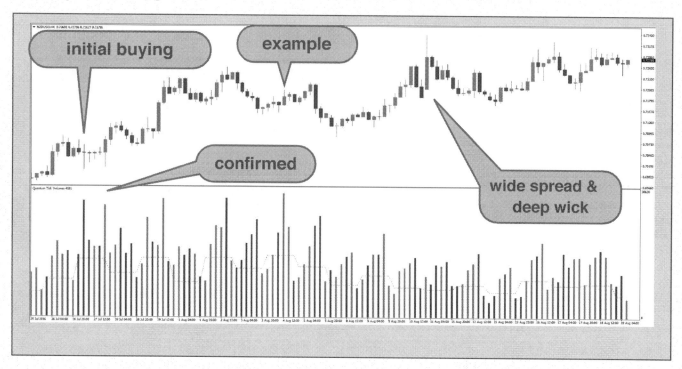

And so to one of the commodity currencies, and if we start at the left of the chart.

Note the initial buying which arrives on the deep hammer candle on high volume on the left, and which is then confirmed in the next session with further buying as denoted by the depth of the wick to the lower body, and on very high volume once more.

This bullish sentiment is then carried forward into the next four hour candle which closes with a wide body, with very small wicks.

Then we see high volume under a narrow spread candle as the pair attempt to continue higher with the market makers selling into weakness here, but the pair turns lower over the next four candles, before an injection of buying once again drives the pair higher in a series of steps, with ultra high volume on the narrower spread candle of the two, hinting at weakness ahead.

Throughout these phases of price action you can spot the anomalous relationships with ease. The simplest place to start is with the highest volume, as this is where our eyes are naturally drawn.

For example, I have highlighted one such on the chart. This is virtually the highest volume of all, and yet look at the price action on the candle. It is very compressed, and with the other volume bars and price candles as benchmarks, we would have to conclude very quickly that this was weakness, with the market makers selling heavily here.

And indeed, even on the 'mini rally' before the bearish engulfing candle, the price action looks weak given the rising volume. Whilst we have rising volume, the price spreads do not reflect the increase in volume, and so signaling the market makers are struggling here and selling into weakness.

And moving to a different example, note the wide spread up candle with the deep wick, yet consider the volume, which is average at best.

Is this a trap?

One would certainly think so, and not yet sprung either. So here we are trading in the range of this candle for the remainder of the chart, and note how many attempts have been made to breach the high of this candle.

Strong resistance is building here, and given the trap move that has now been created, one wonders how much longer it will be before we see the pair sell off strongly.

USD/JPY - 4 hour

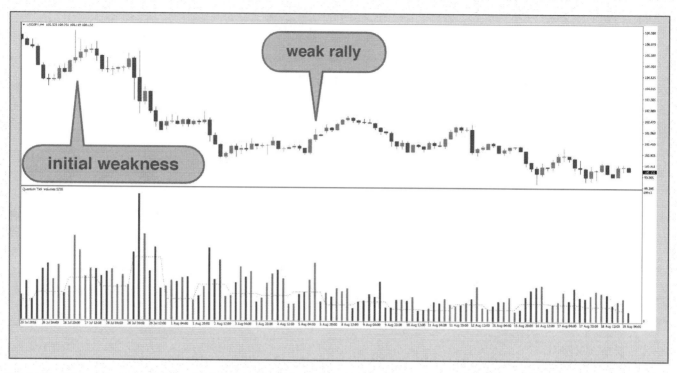

This is a further example of the 'delayed reaction' effect, here with the USD/JPY.

The initial weakness appears to the left of the chart with the high volume and shooting star candle. This is repeated, and confirms the weakness, so eight hours of selling effort here by the market makers.

The market then moves into congestion over the next session, and following on then delivers selling with ultra high volume and a deep wick candle on volatility.

This sentiment then continues following the extended congestion phase, taking the pair down to the floor of the trend.

More congestion follows, before an attempt to rally that is relatively weak, and this is where the yardstick of volume over the chart will help to contextualize the volume. It is more difficult here given the seasonal aspect, but I'm sure you get the general picture.

My Notes

USD/CAD - 4 hour

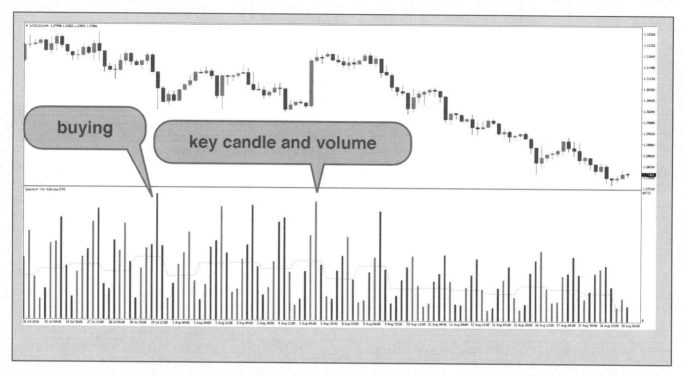

Here we have some more interesting price action, and if we begin with the first candle on the chart at the extreme left This is our first signal of possible weakness with high volume on the shooting star candle, as the market makers sell.

Congestion then follows, but note how we are seeing volume driven in, with no reaction higher with both two bar reversals and also doji candles.

The pair is generally weak, and the bearish tone is one of sliding lower, rather than moving with momentum.

Indeed on the highest volume of the period, the market makers step in to buy this weakness with the deep wick to the lower body of the candle, with the pair rallying, but once again running out of steam and into exhaustion.

The sideways price action continues before we reach the most significant candle and bar on the chart to the centre.

First we see a very wide up spread candle on high volume.

No doubt many traders jump in here expecting a follow through and break through the ceiling of resistance. But the next candle then delivers the real message. There is weakness to come. A huge volume bar with very narrow spread price action.

This signal would be truly hard to miss, and perhaps the hardest part of trading this timeframe is remaining patient, and waiting for this to take effect, because the price action that follows is over two days.

But as we can see from the ensuing price waterfall it was worth the wait, and a very traditional price waterfall then extends over several sessions.

Much of the driver here was a rise in oil price rather than weakness in the US dollar, but both were working in unison to produce this move. Note also how the resistance level held firm throughout, giving us another piece of the puzzle.

An excellent example, which describes the delayed response so typical of the four hour chart.

EUR/CHF - 4 hour

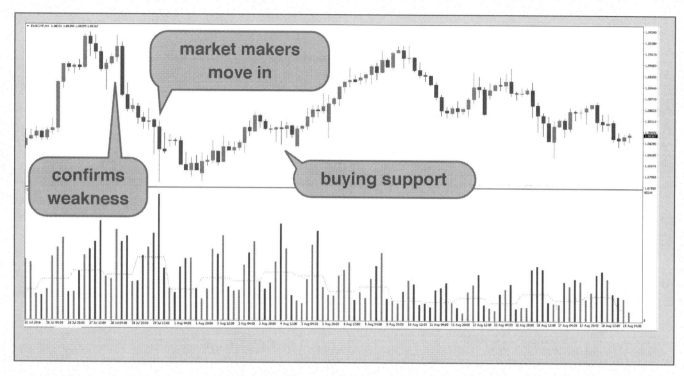

A great example that once again highlights how you have to read the four hour chart. And this one is particularly interesting.

If we start with the first few periods on the left of the chart, here we see the pair rising, and picking up the bullish momentum with some nice wide spread up candle on rising volume.

The final wide spread up candle following the brief congestion period however is on lower volume, and when compared with the first few candles hints at weakness to come.

Bearish sentiment then follows over three down candles, before we see a reaction higher on three up candles, but on the third candle in this sequence higher, a deep wick forms to the upper body on high volume and confirms the weakness, with a wide spread down candle then following which also injects momentum and volume in the move lower.

The selling then begins in earnest, with rising volume over the two sessions before clear stopping volume arrives on the ultra high down candle with the deep wick to the lower body, having been signaled initially on the preceding candle.

The market makers are moving in and buying. Here we see classic stopping volume in action.

But note the rally does not start immediately, and this is the same as other timeframes.

The absorption takes time, and here time is extended across the sessions.

The rally begins, and at the first consolidation phase buying support arrives to prepare for the second phase upwards to the top.

But volume is insufficient to breach the resistance level, which caps the advance, as the pair rolls over on reduced seasonal volumes.

AUD/NZD - 4 hour

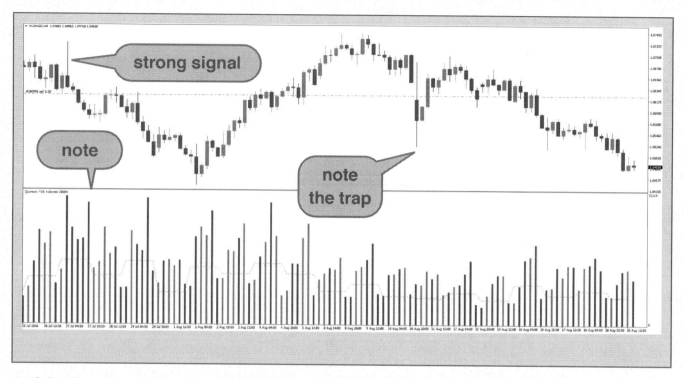

And finally on the four hour timeframe, I have included the AUD/NZD as this is an example of a cross pair where the focus is primarily in the Asia and Far East session.

Once again the delayed aspect is clear with the strong signal of weakness arriving early on the chart with the deep wick candle on very high volume which duly delivers. Note the volume five bars later as the move is brought to a halt before resuming in subsequent sessions.

Selling pressure subsides before we move into the uptrend, which is driven higher on good volume as the sessions unfold. Then we reach an interesting phase of price action. Note the volatile candle, but check out the volume - it is very, very low here.

The market makers are not participating so any move away from here is likely to be a trap. And so it proves! The rally higher is short, before the downwards trend develops with the pair continuing to remain bearish longer term.

And as you can see on this chart I do have a live order in the market on this pair, and likely to add further to the position if it develops by scaling in.

My Notes

Section Six - Currency futures

In this final section I want to consider several examples from the world of currency futures, and in a variety of timeframes.

As you will see, volume price analysis applies equally well here, and here the insiders are the big operators.

The only complication we have in the world of currency futures, every currency is quoted against the US dollar.

So the USD/CAD becomes the CAD/USD and the USD/JPY becomes the JPY/USD, and all the chart examples here are from NinjaTrader.

Worked

Examples

6A - (AUD/USD) 10 minute chart

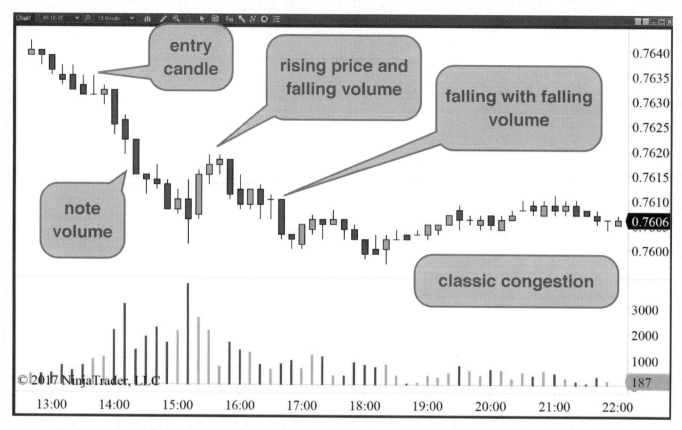

And we start with the 6A which is the futures contract for the Aussie dollar on a fast timeframe, and this is a ten minute chart. The period here is from the start of the US session as this gets underway, and through to the close, so we are comparing apples with apples here in terms of volume.

As we get underway to the left of the chart, the pair remains bearish, and is moving firmly lower on rising volume, and note the nice entry candle on the first pause point, which is followed two candles later by an injection of both momentum and volume.

However, what is interesting in the next wide spread down candle is the reduction in volume when compared to the one earlier, and this sends us a signal that selling pressure is waning. Why? Because, we should expect to see the same volume here.

We do not, and it is also substantially lower than the previous candle, so the big operators are stepping back here. And so it proves to be, as they move into the market strongly just after 15.00 on a news release.

However, whether this is buying or selling is less clear with the pair rising over three candles, but this still looks weak for two reasons. First, the volume is falling as the market rises, and second the spreads are narrowing so suggesting further weakness to come.

The pair then rolls over, and once again note the volume here, it is falling with a falling market, so this confirms the selling pressure is no longer dominant.

And so we move into the classic congestion phase of narrow spread candles in a narrow range, and with volume falling away as the big operators withdraw, and move on to another pair.

6A - (AUD/USD) 15 minute chart

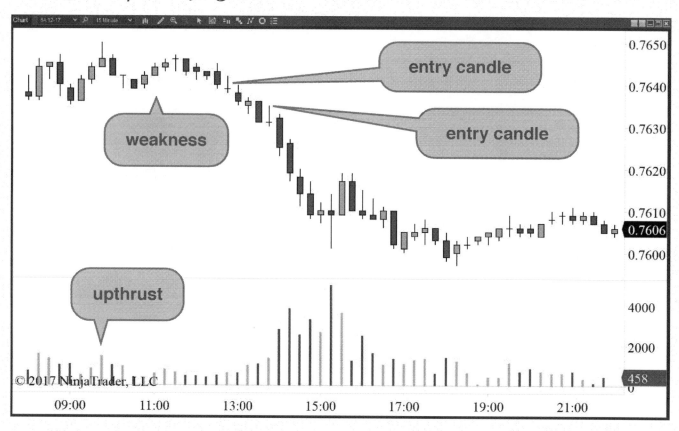

I thought it would be interesting to consider the same price action for the 6A on a slightly slower timeframe, and encompassing both the London and US sessions.

So this chart broadly covers the market from the London open to the close of the US session, and in doing so also gives us a very different perspective on the reaction to news at 15.00.

And once again here, we do have to remember, that until the surge in volume at the centre of the chart, the preceding volume bars would have been much more descriptive.

So in considering this chart, please do not think the volume to the left cannot be read. It can, and the volume spikes in the London session would have been just as meaningful.

As I mentioned in the previous example, the pair had been signaling weakness throughout the London session with constant efforts to rise, all of which failed to hold above the strong ceiling of resistance.

Note the upthrust on high volume and the weak rally on narrow spreads followed by the hanging man.

All signs of weakness with the US session then picking up the bearish momentum, and into the price waterfall. As you can see we also have some excellent 'entry' candles here too.

And so down to the highest volume of the day, and here too we have indecision with the long legged doji candle, and just confirming what we have seen on the ten minute chart.

The pair rallies, but the immediate reversal suggests weakness on the two bar reversal, and confirms what we have seen on the faster chart with some further weakness here on the subsequent two candles.

6B - (GBP/USD) 30 minute chart

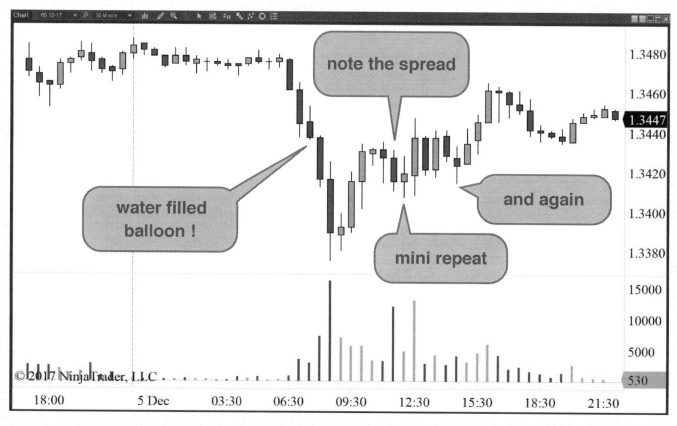

This is an interesting example from the 30 minute chart for the British pound, and once again demonstrates the importance of comparing volume in the sessions. This period of price action covers the market from the mid to late US session on the left, then moves into the Far East and Asia session.

Towards the centre of the chart we see London enter, and get underway before we move across the chart into a second US session to the close. This gives us a sense of the how the volumes vary from one session to another.

The price waterfall here is classic, with rising volume as the pair falls strongly, and note the weak attempt to rally on candle three in the sequence. This is the balloon filling with water which then bursts, and off we go again.

The dramatic volume at the bottom signals a big move by the big operators, and suggests strong buying, but we have to wait for the next candle for a clearer signal, which again, is perhaps not so clear, because this could simply be a pause point.

The doji tells us there is indecision, but we cannot be sure on the direction at this point so again patience is required.

The subsequent candle does then confirm with a clean wide spread up candle on excellent volume, and up we go and into the congestion phase.

Note how we see the down candle on extremely high volume which fails to follow through. This is almost a mini repeat of earlier, and given the volume we would have expected to see a much wider candle.

Compare this to earlier where we have wider spread candles on much higher volume. This suggests the big operators are buying, and so the price is contained. There is another even smaller repeat of this later in this phase of price action before the pair finally break higher on rising volume.

6B - (GBP/USD) monthly chart

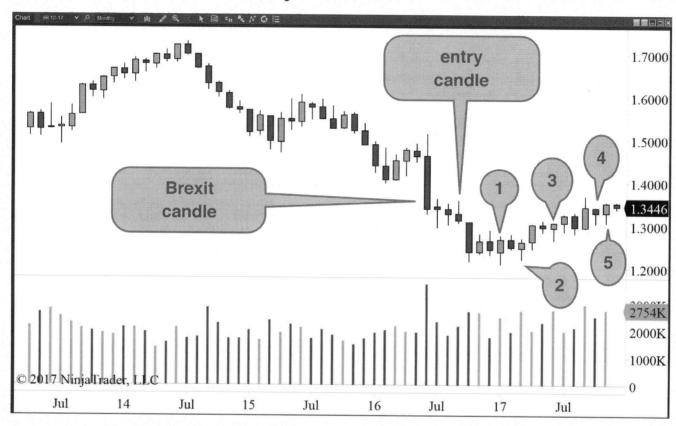

And here we have moved to a much slower timeframe for the 6B, which I thought would be interesting as this also embraces the shock vote by the UK to exit the EU which occurred in 2016. The period here is almost five years, from April 2013 through to December 2017.

The Brexit candle is the one to the right of the chart, and has the heaviest volume, and given the lack of buying, as denoted by the lack of any wick to the lower body, it was no surprise to see this very bearish sentiment continue for the next four months. And as you can see, once again we have a nice entry candle with October delivering further bearish sentiment.

Then we move into the inevitable accumulation phase, and remember this was also reinforced with much market commentary and analysis suggesting that perhaps the reaction was overdone, and that the UK economy would survive and perhaps even prosper after all! The world was not about to end.

Remember too, the reaction for the British pound was universal across the complex with heavy and sustained selling in all the pound pairs. In addition, this was also reflected in risk assets with gold soaring, very strong Swiss franc and yen flows, and a selling of equities worldwide.

This event really did rock the global boat. Since then the waters have calmed, and we have seen the classic accumulation phase developing, with the big operators taking advantage of each and every piece of news, as the GBP lurches this way and that on positive and negative Brexit news, that is constant and unrelenting.

And note the four buying phases (accumulation), with a fifth just built in November (1 - 5). In addition we are also breaking through resistance in the 1.3300 area which has now become support.

6C - (CAD/USD) 15 minute chart

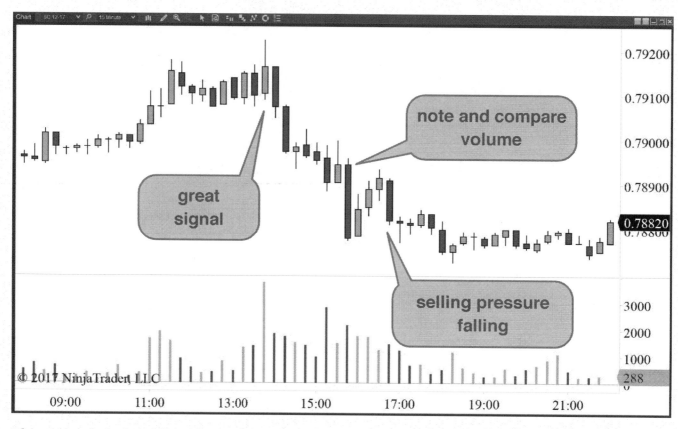

This example is from the other end of the spectrum, and is the 6C contract on a fifteen minute timeframe.

And remember, that in the world of futures the quoting convention is for the USD always to be the counter currency. In other words, the second currency quoted, so this is reversed from the spot currency notation, and is the CAD/USD, not the other way round.

The chart covers the session from the London open to the US close.

And we have some more 'water filled ballon candles' here! If we start with the highest volume of the session, this is a great signal and really the only question is whether you get in early, or wait for the bearish trend to develop.

Two wide spread down candles follow with one confirming the other on similar volume, before we move into the congestion phase which slides lower before accelerating on high volume, followed by a further weak up candle with a well developed wick and down to the next phase.

However note the volume under the final wide spread down candle in this move, it is modest compared to the others in this session and signals the bearish selling pressure is perhaps waning, and coming to an end.

This is further confirmed by the down candle four candles later, which is also has a wide spread, but the volume is substantially lower. In addition, this is back within a range of price which has seen heavy selling four candles earlier, suggesting selling pressure is indeed diminishing.

This certainly seems to be the case as we move to the close with some bullish sentiment returning, and a strong platform of support building, which may then provide the platform for a bounce higher.

6E - (EUR/USD) 5 minute chart

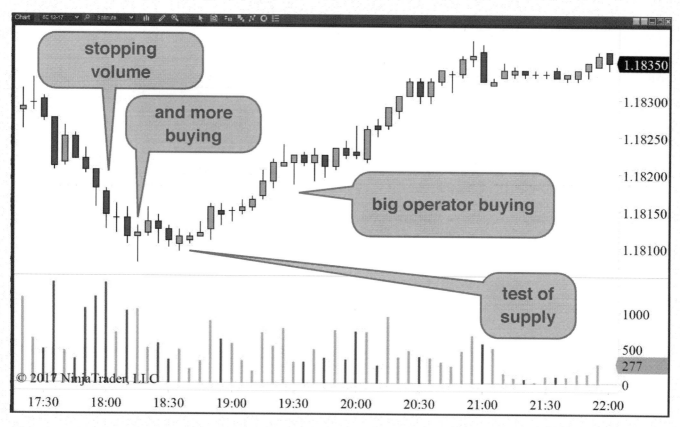

The euro dollar is everyone's favourite pair and here we have the 6E on a 5 minute chart. The period here is from late morning in the US session through to the close.

And if we start with the first candle on the chart, which is a long legged doji candle giving us a signal of indecision, which is then followed by the classic shooting star candle, but on average volume.

Not a strong signal.

Nor indeed is the next candle, a narrow spread down candle on even lower volume, so at this point, there is very little to suggest a strong move in one direction or another.

Then we see the next candle which is wide spread and down on very high volume.

The big operators are selling, and the following candle, although closing as an up candle, looks very weak on very low volume, which is validated as the price waterfall develops.

Then we start to see rising volume, but note the wicks developing to the lower body of the candles, signaling stopping volume is building as the big operators begin to move in and buy, with further buying in the hammer candle at the bottom.

The pair then moves into congestion before we see a test of supply and off we go with some well developed momentum.

The congestion phase is also interesting with further big operator support and buying arriving here, so driving the pair up to the next level, before volume drains away as we prepare for the Far East and Asia session where focus shifts from European currencies and the US dollar, to the commodity currencies and the Japanese yen.

6J - (JPY/USD) monthly chart

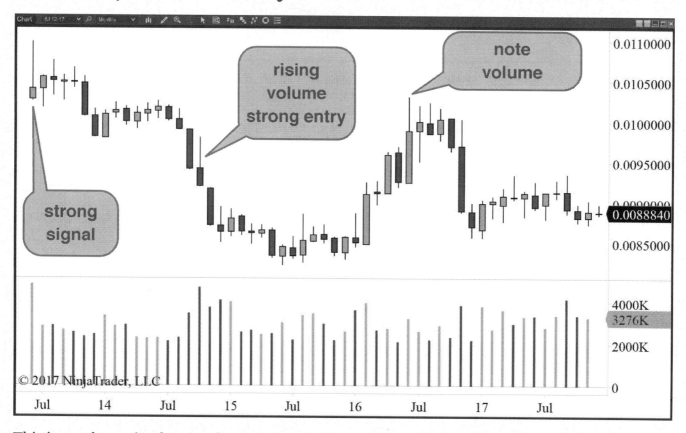

This is another pair where we have to reverse the notation, this time for the JPY/USD, a notoriously tricky pair to trade, but one where considering the slower timeframes will always help to frame the current price action.

Here I have chosen the monthly chart, but a daily or weekly chart would be just as useful. Of course, signals here require patience, and the first arrives immediately on the first candle as the big operators sell very heavily here.

The move lower begins, but note the rally higher and the volume on the second candle. This looks weak as indeed do the subsequent candles.

Then the selling starts in earnest as the price waterfall develops on rising volume, before we reach the congestion phase and accumulation with several gravestone doji candles here.

The rally higher begins on high volume, but note the final wide spread up candle in the rally, and more particularly the associated volume and wick to the upper body.

The volume looks low, and the wick suggests weakness, and coupled with the fact that this price level is now testing resistance above it's no surprise to see this level hold firm, before bearish sentiment takes hold once more.

The current phase of congestion is now also looking increasingly fragile, with repeated efforts to rise all failing, and on increasing volume on the most recent candle.

My other books

ANNA COULLING

A Complete Guide to Volume Price Analysis

Read the book then read the market

In the UK we have a product called Marmite. It is a deeply divisive food, which you either love or hate. Those who love it, cannot understand how anyone could live without it - and of course, the opposite is true for those who hate it! This sentiment could be applied to volume as a trading indicator.

In other words, you are likely to fall into one of two camps. You either believe it works, or you don't. It really is that simple. There is no halfway house here! I make no bones about the fact that I believe I was lucky in starting my own trading journey using volume.

To me it just made sense, and the logic of what it revealed was inescapable. And for me, the most powerful reason is very simple. Volume is a rare commodity in trading because it is a leading indicator. The second, and only other leading indicator, is price.

As traders, investors or speculators, all we are trying to do is to anticipate where the market is heading next. So is there any better way than to use the only two leading indicators we have at our disposal, namely volume and price? In isolation each tells us very little. After all, volume is just that, no more no less. A price is a price. However, combine these two forces together, and the result is a powerful analytical approach to anticipating market direction.

However, as I say at the start of the book, there is nothing new in trading, as the analysis of volume has been around for over 100 years. After all, this is where the iconic traders started. Traders such as Charles Dow, Jesse Livermore, Richard Wyckoff, and Richard Ney. All they had was the ticker tape, from which they read the price, and the number of shares traded. In other words, Volume Price Analysis (VPA), short and simple.

The book has been written for traders and investors who have never come across this methodology, and also for those who have some knowledge, and perhaps wish to learn a little more. It is not revolutionary, or innovative, but just simple sound common sense, combined with logic. And here is a typical comment from one of my readers:

"I loved your book on VPA. I have read many books on the markets but yours was the only one that generated an 'aha' moment for me. I have deployed VPA in my trading strategies and I have been delighted with the results."

This is just one of the many hundreds of emails I have received since writing the book, and you can read more on Amazon where it is a number one best seller.

More information at www.annacoulling.com

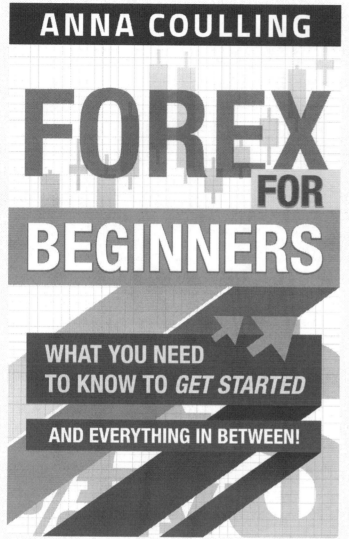

There are of course many books about forex trading. What is different about this book, is the focus on those aspects of trading which I believe are fundamental. After all, there are only two questions we need to answer when considering a position in the market:-

What is the likely outcome on this trade, and what is my confidence in my analysis - high, medium or low?

And what is the financial risk on this trade?

The first is the hardest question to answer, and the book will explain in detail the analysis and approach to use, in order to answer this question with confidence.

The second question is more straightforward and is answered provided you have an understanding of risk, money management and position sizing in relation to your trading capital. Again, this is covered in detail in the book. As the tag line on the front cover says 'What you need to know to get started, and everything in between' which really sums up what you will learn.

The book explains everything, from the pure mechanics to the trading methodology that I advocate, and which I have used in all my own trading and investing for over 20 years. Forex For Beginners is also dedicated to all those traders who have asked me to write such an introduction, based on my knowledge and my methodology.

More information at www.annacoulling.com

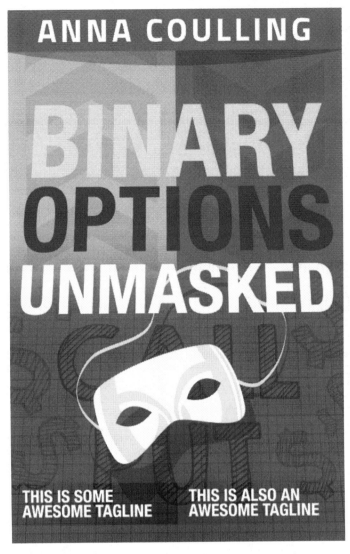

ANNA COULLING

BINARY OPTIONS UNMASKED

THIS IS SOME AWESOME TAGLINE   THIS IS ALSO AN AWESOME TAGLINE

Binary options - is it betting or trading? A debate that has been raging ever since binary options exploded onto the market, sweeping away convention, tearing up the rulebook, and dividing opinion. Indeed, simply mention the word binary and instantly a heated debate will ensue. But love them or loathe them, binary options are here to stay, and Binary Options Unmasked has been written to provide traders with a balanced and considered view of these deceptively simple yet powerful instruments. There are many traps for the unwary, but there are also some solid gold nuggets, if you know where to look.

So are binary options for me? This is the question I hope will be answered for you in this book. In writing it, I have tried to provide a complete introduction to the subject, with practical examples of how to approach these innovative instruments. Every aspect of this market is explained - both the good, and the bad. Nothing is left unsaid. Binary options have much to offer, and used with common sense and thought, are perfectly valid trading instruments. Applied unthinkingly, they become like any other instrument - a quick way to lose money fast.

Binary Options Unmasked reveals the true characteristics of this market. It covers the current market participants, along with their product offering. Moreover, not only are binary options explained in detail, but their application as a trading instrument is also illustrated. Trading strategies and approaches too are explored, along with an innovative and practical approach to interpreting volatility, a key component of any options trading. I hope this book, will give you the confidence at least to consider these instruments in more detail for yourself, with an open mind and your eyes wide open.

More information at www.annacoulling.com

ANNA COULLING

A

Three Dimensional Approach to Forex Trading

Answers the question –
where is the market going next?

Using the power of
RELATIONAL, FUNDAMENTAL
and TECHNICAL analysis

If you aspire to becoming a full time forex trader, then this is the book for you. Even if your dream is perhaps more modest, and you simply want to have a second income trading the forex markets, then again, this book is for you.

And perhaps you have some questions such as:-

What will I learn?

How will it help me?

So let me answer those for you.

The book has been written with one clear objective. To explain how and why the currency markets move in the way they do - the forces, the factors and the manipulators.

Many aspiring traders, simply do not realize that the forex market sits at the heart of the financial world, which when you think about it logically, is really common sense. After all, this is the biggest money market in the world, and if the financial markets are about one thing, they are about money. Making it, protecting it, or increasing the return.

It's no surprise therefore, the forex market connects all the others. Put simply, the forex market is the ultimate barometer of risk.

So how will this book help me to become a better forex trader? Well, in several ways!

First, you will discover how changes in market sentiment in the primary markets of commodities, stocks, bonds and equities, are then reflected in the currency markets. This is something which often surprises novice traders. After all, why look at a stock index, or the price of gold, or a bond market? The answer is very simple. It is in these markets that you will find all the clues and signals, which then reveal money flow. After all, the financial markets are all about risk. In other words, higher returns for higher risk, or lower returns for lower risk.

It really is that simple. And yet, how many forex traders ever consider associated markets? And the answer is very few. After reading the book, you will be one of those enlightened traders who truly understands money flow and risk, and your confidence as a trader will grow exponentially as a result.

The next thing you will learn is that trading in one dimension or using one trading technique, is rather limiting. You have probably met people who trade, who then make a bold statement such as: 'I only trade using the fundamentals' or perhaps that 'technical analysis is a self fulfilling prophecy'. To trade successfully in the forex world requires a three dimensional approach which embraces the fundamental, the relational and the technical and is what this book is all about.

More information at www.annacoulling.com

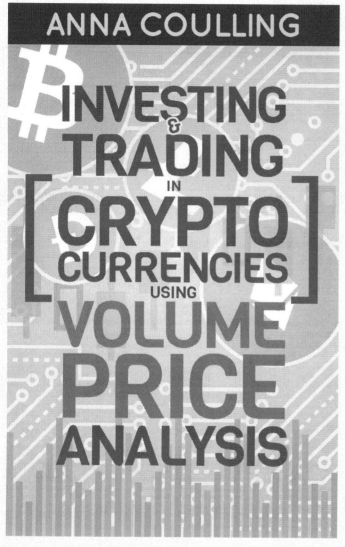

ANNA COULLING

INVESTING & TRADING IN [CRYPTO CURRENCIES] USING VOLUME PRICE ANALYSIS

If you have not yet discovered the world of cryptocurrencies, in the next few years you almost certainly will, as they are the latest phenomenon to take the financial markets by storm. And they follow in the footsteps of binary options.

But like all new instruments and markets, there are many pitfalls and traps for the unwary, and even more so here. And for many reasons.

First, we have an unregulated market, and one which has no central exchange with no transparency, and little in the way of investor protection. Second, we have a group of instruments that are extremely volatile. Third, none of the major regulators have been able to agree on how to classify and regulate this instrument, with some suggesting it is an asset, others a commodity, and to some a currency.

Finally, and perhaps most worryingly of all, hundreds of new cryptocurrencies are being launched weekly, adding to a market that is already chaotic and largely driven by the fear of missing out. Many have already suggested this is nothing more than a replica of the dot com bubble or tulip mania, and one which will all end in tears.

So, what are the facts? Should you even consider this market, either as an investor, speculator or trader? And if so, how you can make logical common sense investment or trading decisions in such an uncertain market.

In this book, I aim to show you how, whether your purpose is to invest for the longer term, or to trade the markets intraday. And the only approach which can give you the insight to anticipate future market direction with confidence for cryptocurrencies, is by application of volume price analysis.

In the world of cryptocurrencies, volume represents the buyers and sellers in the market, and so takes us directly to the heart of supply and demand, as described in Wyckoff's first law.

The application of volume price analysis can be traced back to the iconic traders of the past. Trading greats such as Charles Dow, Jesse Livermore, Richard Wyckoff and Richard Ney. All used volume and price to build their fortunes.

Today, we have brought this methodology up to date, and based it on the codified laws of Richard Wyckoff. Here you will find over 100 worked examples in all timeframes and for a variety of the most popular cryptocurrencies, clearly annotated and with detailed descriptions, to demonstrate how you can leverage the power of volume price analysis for trading this market.

And better still, it is an approach you can apply to your existing trading style. There is no need to change or abandon your existing approach, something many of my readers have confirmed with their public comments on my other books on Amazon.

So if you are considering entering the world of cryptocurrencies, grab your copy now. Here you will find out what they are, and perhaps what they are not. And just as important, where the opportunities are to be found, and how to take advantage.

More information at www.annacoulling.com

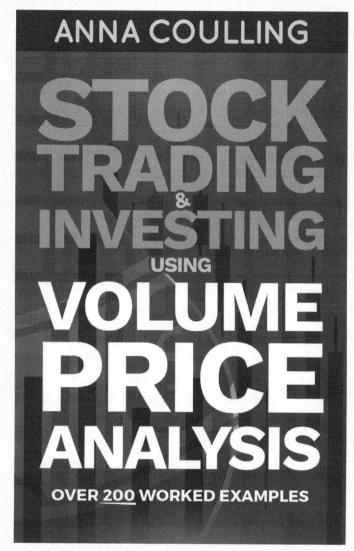

ANNA COULLING

STOCK TRADING & INVESTING USING VOLUME PRICE ANALYSIS

OVER 200 WORKED EXAMPLES

In this book of over 200 worked examples for stock traders and investors, you will discover an approach that was used by the iconic traders of the past to build their vast fortunes.

Traders such as Jesse Livermore, Richard Wyckoff and Richard Ney all succeeded because they understood the power of the tape which delivered just two key pieces of information, namely volume and price, and from which they were able to anticipate where the market was going next.

This approach was also codified by Richard Wyckoff into three principle laws, and forms the basis of volume price analysis. It is a powerful methodology that can be applied to all markets, instruments and timeframes regardless of whether you are an investor, trader or speculator.

The examples presented in this book are drawn primarily from US stock markets, but also includes examples taken from the futures markets, such as indices, commodities, currency futures and bonds.

Each chart example is fully annotated to illustrate and highlight key points in the associated text, and together provide a detailed and comprehensive study of the volume price relationship, and giving clear signals as to where the stock is going next.

And regardless of whether you are selecting stocks for growth, dividend yield, option strategies, or for speculative day trading, volume price analysis will highlight which ones to buy or sell, and when.

Armed with this knowledge, success awaits.

More information at www.annacoulling.com

Thank you & acknowledgements

Thank you for investing in this book and I hope you have found the worked examples helpful in expanding your knowledge and understanding of volume price analysis.

If you would like to discover more of my work, you can find me on my personal site at http://www.annacoulling.com where I write regular market analysis using volume price analysis across all the markets. There you will find my Facebook pages and also my Twitter feed which is http://twitter.com/annacoull and below are details of my other books which are all available on Amazon both in Kindle format and as paperbacks :

A Complete Guide To Volume Price Analysis

Forex For Beginners

A Three Dimensional Approach To Forex Trading

Binary Options Unmasked

Stock Trading & Investing Using Volume Price Analysis

Forex Trading Using Volume Price Analysis

Investing & Trading in Cryptocurrencies Using Volume Price Analysis

I'm also the founder of Quantum Trading along with my husband and trading partner David, and at Quantum Trading you will find a range of tools and indicators developed by us for traders and investors. You will also find indicators such as the Volume Point Of Control which develops the idea of volume to embrace the volume/price/ time relationship on the Y axis of the price chart, thereby creating a very different view of support and resistance based on the principles of market profile and the value area. And you can find all the details here. The indicators are currently available for MT4, MT5 and NinjaTrader. However, we are also working on other platforms such as Tradestation and Multicharts.

http://www.quantumtrading.com

You may also be interested to know that David and I have developed a complete course of education for aspiring forex traders, and this is called The Complete Forex Trading Program. The program includes the full suite of tools and indicators from Quantum Trading along with a comprehensive online learning resource of videos and video podcasts to help you understand all you need to know to succeed in this uncompromising market.

All the details are here:

http://www.quantumtradingeducation.com

For stock investors and traders my personal site is regularly updated with my analysis of the primary indices and individual stocks based on volume price analysis. Here you will also be able to join me in live market sessions where I am joined by my husband and trading partner, where we analyse stock charts from various markets around the world, and using volume price analysis once again. You can find all the details here:

http://www.annacoulling.com

Finally I would like to thank NinjaTrader and MetaQuotes for allowing me to use charts using their platform. Many of the chart examples in this book are from my NinjaTrader trading platform. The NinjaTrader platform with the Kinetick data feed is one of the most powerful combinations in the market, and is available on a free, end of day basis.

You can find further details on the platform and feeds at http://www.ninjatrader.com

The MT4 and MT5 platforms are the most popular trading platforms in the world and are the perfect place to get started if you are new to the trading world. You can find all the details at

https://www.metatrader4.com/

Finally it only remains for me to wish you every success and good fortune in your own trading,

Kindest regards

Anna

I would kindly request you do not share, distribute, publish or copy any of this material in any way, as you will then be in breach of my copyright.

Thank you for protecting my work.

Made in the USA
Middletown, DE
04 February 2020